LINCOLN AND THE FIRST SHOT

Lincoln and the First Shot

RICHARD N. CURRENT

WAVELAND
PRESS, INC.
Prospect Heights, Illinois

For information about this book, write or call:

Waveland Press, Inc.
P.O. Box 400
Prospect Heights, Illinois 60070
(847) 634-0081

7

To my brother Ira

FOREWORD

"Our arms will never be used to strike the first blow in any attack," President John F. Kennedy declared in January, 1961. "It is our national tradition."[1] *

By the time Kennedy spoke, the technology of war had been developed to the point where, under conceivable circumstances, it might seem like national suicide for the United States to wait for an enemy to strike first. Nuclear weapons with the explosive power of many megatons, together with intercontinental ballistic missiles to deliver them, apparently could come close to making the first blow the last and decisive one. Yet spokesmen for the American government continued to stress the second-strike rather than the first-strike capabilities and intentions of the United States.[2]

The "national tradition," as Kennedy called it, was both long and strong. It drew its strength, no doubt, from certain distinctive elements of American democracy itself. According to the democratic ideal, the people are by nature peaceably inclined, and so are their leaders, the government being presumably under popular control. The people will resent insults and repel

* Superior figures refer to the section of Notes at the end of the book.

dangers, but they will not take the initiative in starting a war.

To some extent, political realities have coincided with democratic assumptions. Americans have been remarkably heterogeneous in their ethnic origins, in their geographic conditions and sectional attachments, and in their economic and religious interests. They have been unusually individualistic, without institutional loyalties to herd them, and independent, without the habit of obedience to or even recognition of hereditary superiors. With peace as the ideal and diversity as the fact, the people have not been willing to combine for the hardships and sacrifices of war except when convinced that someone, deliberately, satanically, has struck at them, their government, its symbols, or the ideal of peace. Only then have Americans come together to take up the battle, with patriotism and fighting spirit.

But, even then, the response has not always been unanimous. On occasion, dissenters have come forth to question whether the enemy's seeming act of aggression was quite genuine. Some of them have gone on to charge that, somehow, the president himself has either invented or contrived the announced attack. Indeed, the men in office, if they had motives for war, would also have reasons for making it appear that war had been forced upon them. If it did not appear so, they would meet extraordinary difficulty in rousing sufficient popular support.

Certainly the war presidents of recent times have

taken pains to demonstrate that they did not make war upon another country but only accepted the war which the other country was already making upon their own. In 1941, after his war council had discussed the aggressive program of the Japanese and ways to "maneuver them into the position of firing the first shot," Franklin D. Roosevelt needed to wait no longer when the Japanese suddenly raided Pearl Harbor. In 1917, with the *Lusitania* incident in the background, Woodrow Wilson emphasized Germany's renewal of unrestricted submarine warfare as tantamount to the waging of war by Germany against the United States. In 1898, asking for the means to restore peace, not to make war, William McKinley spoke to a Congress and a public who remembered the *Maine*.

The tradition that the enemy must strike first—and the belief that he always has done so—goes back to the beginning of the very first of distinctly American wars, the War of Independence. On that historic April 19, 1775, as patriots believed, the redcoat Major Pitcairn with his regulars approached the Minutemen innocently assembled on the Lexington green, curtly told them, "Disperse, ye rebels!" and then wantonly ordered his men to fire. In 1812 Americans again went to war with Great Britain because, as they saw it, Great Britain was guilty of deliberate aggression. For years the British had been impressing American sailors and interfering with American trade. His Majesty's Ship the *Leopard* had even fired upon a United States war vessel, the *Chesapeake*, and though this happened five years before Congress got around to declaring war, the incident was, in one sense, the "Pearl Harbor" of the War of 1812.

In 1846, having ordered an army into disputed territory along the Rio Grande, James K. Polk asked Congress for a declaration of war after the troops had been fired upon. War exists, he said, and by the act of Mexico herself. "American blood has been shed upon American soil." Polk was the first president to be accused of deliberately bringing about an attack, or the semblance of an attack, in order to rouse the American people and lead them to war.

One of the most pointed and persistent of Polk's accusers was Abraham Lincoln. As a congressman during the Mexican War, Lincoln repeatedly introduced his "spot resolutions," by which he intended to show that the spot where the blood had been shed was not on American soil at all. He averred that the war had come in consequence of Polk's manipulations rather than Mexican threats or aggressions. In after years Lincoln did not forget his accusation against Polk. As late as June, 1860, he repeated it in material he provided for a campaign biography. As he then phrased the charge, "the President had sent Genl. Taylor into an uninhabited part of the country belonging to Mexico, and not to the U. S. and thereby had provoked the first act of hostility." The President had sought war, Lincoln added, for an ulterior motive of politics, that is, "to divert public attention" from his failure to secure from Great Britain the whole of the Oregon country, which his own fellow partisans had been demanding.[3]

There is more than a bit of irony in Lincoln's accusation against Polk. Within half a year of reviving it, Lincoln as president was himself to face the question of sending armed forces into disputed territory, and eventually his decision was to make him the second president to be charged with contriving a war and shifting the guilt to the other side.

Since 1861 much more has been written, pro and con, about Lincoln's Sumter policy than about Polk's dealings with Mexico. Since 1941, it is true, the controversy regarding Lincoln and Fort Sumter has had to compete for attention with the controversy regarding Roosevelt and Pearl Harbor.[4] But the Sumter question continues to attract and intrigue students of American history. It does so for a number of reasons. It reflects, and in turn casts light upon, the national tradition of avoiding the "first shot." It concerns the events that led directly to the Civil War, the greatest of wars from the American point of view. And it involves problems of historical evidence and interpretation which have more fascination than even the best of ordinary puzzles.

The following account does not claim to provide the final solution. It does not even pretend (though it does aspire) to be entirely free from the errors of fact which have found their way into most writings on the subject. It does attempt to correct more old errors than the new ones it makes, and to add at least a little to the interest in and understanding of what Lincoln actually tried to do, and did, in March and April, 1861.

Foreword

In the preparation of this book I have been helped, in one way or another, by my friends Fred H. Harrington, William B. Hesseltine, Kenneth M. Stampp, T. Harry Williams, and William A. Williams, and by my wife Rose B. Current. My deepest thanks go to all of them. I have also learned a great deal from my friends David M. Potter and the late J. G. Randall. My disagreements with these two distinguished scholars, at various points in the Sumter story, are not to be taken as marks of disrespect, even in the slightest, for them or for their contributions to the understanding of the subject.

R. N. C.

Oxford, England

CONTENTS

1. Determination

1

THE six o'clock train from Philadelphia came to a halt, the locomotive steaming in the chill of the February dawn. A tall man, conspicuous among the other passengers only because of his height, stepped down from the cars. He was casually dressed, with a muffler, a heavy jacket, and a soft slouch hat. Beside him walked two companions, one a burly fellow who tried not to look like a bodyguard, the other a man with the wary tread of a detective pretending to be an ordinary traveler.

Unannounced, ahead of schedule, furtive. This was no proper way for a president-elect of the United States to make his appearance in the nation's capital. He ought not to sneak in! And always afterward Abraham Lincoln regretted that he had allowed himself to be talked into doing so.

True, there appeared to be reason enough for caution, even for excessive caution. Not all Americans were willing to accept Lincoln, the "Black Republican," as their chief executive. Some hated him enough to kill him.

Already the seven slave states of the Lower South

had made his election the occasion for seceding and setting up a rival government, with a president of their own. They had seized almost all the Federal post offices, customs houses, mints, arsenals, and forts that lay within their boundaries, and they were demanding the surrender of the few forts that still were garrisoned by United States troops. One of these few—Fort Sumter, off Charleston, South Carolina—had become the focus of attention, North and South. An incident there might bring violence at any minute.

The other eight slave states, those of the Upper South and the border, stood in precarious balance between the free states of the old Union and the slave states of the new Confederacy. If the eight should join the seven already gone, the Union would be reduced to a sorry remnant, even with its remaining eighteen free states. If, among the eight, Virginia should secede, others would undoubtedly follow. And if Maryland were to go, the Union remnant would have lost the overland approach to its own capital.

Thus, at the time when Lincoln arrived in Washington, he and the city and the nation faced the prospect of multiplying calamities. For months, hot-headed secessionists in Virginia had been urging, openly as well as secretly, that Virginians and Marylanders stage a coup, get control of Washington, and prevent the inauguration of the new president. According to rumor, the secessionists even plotted to assassinate him, on his way through Baltimore.

On account of this rumor, Lincoln had been persuaded to leave Pennsylvania hastily, at night, instead of waiting with his family for the train that had been scheduled to take him, the next day, to Washington. The case for caution had been reasonable: the survival of the Union might well depend on the safety of the incoming president. Yet, by avoiding the risk to his life, Lincoln incurred a risk to his reputation, the risk of giving an impression of weakness, timidity, indecision. Such an impression was, indeed, to be given in unfriendly and exaggerated accounts of his trip to Washington—the last leg of his long, zigzag journey from Springfield, Illinois.

This appearance of pusillanimity did not really fit the facts. Actually, Lincoln was strong, brave, determined. From the beginning of secession he had known what, basically, he was going to do, what he had to do, about the forts and other Federal property in the South. His conviction was on record, in confidential letters, in public speeches.

For the information of the general in chief of the United States Army, Winfield Scott, he had written on the day after the first state, South Carolina, seceded: "Please present my respects to the General, and tell him, confidentially, I shall be obliged to him to be as well prepared as he can to either *hold*, or *retake*, the forts, as the case may require, at and after the inauguration."

Again, the same day: "According to my present view, if the forts shall be given up before the inauguration, the General must retake them afterwards."

And the next day: "The most we can do now is to watch events, and be as well prepared as possible for any turn things may take. If the forts fall, my judgment is that they are to be retaken."

During the weeks that followed, as Lincoln watched events, and one by one most of the forts fell, he came to realize that retaking them would be no mere military enterprise, no simple matter of ordering fleets to sail or armies to march. Not only in the Lower South but throughout the slave states and even in some quarters of the North, it was believed that the Federal government had no constitutional right to use force against a seceding state. Such force, in the language of the day, would be "coercion," and coercion would mean war. It would probably lead to the secession of Virginia and other states. It might even cost Lincoln a large part of his Northern support.

Fully aware of the hazards, Lincoln never publicly proposed coercion as such. Still, in some of the talks he made on the journey from Springfield to Washington, he did not flinch from declaring his determination.

There need be no coercion, he said during his stop in Indianapolis. "But if the Government, for instance, but simply insists upon holding its own forts, or retaking those forts which belong to it,"—here he was interrupted by cheers—"or the enforcement of the laws of the United States in the collection of duties upon foreign importations,"—more cheers—". . . would any or all of these things be coercion?"

Certainly Lincoln did not advocate war. "The man does not live who is more devoted to peace than I am," he said at a later stop, in Trenton. "None who would do more to preserve it. But it may be necessary to put the foot down firmly." The applause was instant and deafening.

There was no occasion for bloodshed, he told his equally enthusiastic listeners at a flag-raising ceremony, on Washington's Birthday, in historic Independence Hall, Philadelphia. "I am not in favor of such a course," he said, "and I may say in advance, there will be no blood shed unless it be forced upon the Government. The Government will not use force unless force is used against it."

He repeated and further qualified this assurance at Harrisburg later the same day, not long before his sudden departure for Washington (by way of Philadelphia). "It shall be my endeavor," he now explained, "to preserve the peace of this country so far as it can be done, consistently with the maintenance of the institutions of the country." Peace, that is, but not at the price of the Union.

Lincoln's remarks en route to Washington reflected some of the passages in the draft of his inaugural address, which, in the form of printed sheets, he carried with him. One passage, as originally set up in type, read: "All the power at my disposal will be used to reclaim the public property and places which have fallen; to hold, occupy and possess these, and all other property and places belonging to the government, and to collect the duties on imports; but beyond what may be necessary for these, there will be no invasion of any State."

There would be no war unless the Southerners started one. "The government will not assail *you*," he had written in an apostrophe to them, "unless you *first* assail it." His concluding line repeated the challenge: "With *you,* and not with *me,* is the solemn question of 'Shall it be peace, or a sword?' "[1]

Just how Lincoln was going to carry out his policy he had not explained in the inaugural draft. He could not yet know precisely how he would manage to do it. Yet do it he would. So he believed as, with firm will, he strode beside the train that had brought him to Washington—and to high responsibility that would be his, alone, in a week and a half.

A bold entrance, despite all peril, would have been in keeping with his position and his resolve, as well as his characteristic disregard of personal danger. Yet here he was, masquerading as a common citizen if not a common criminal, and succeeding in the deception. No one in the railroad station recognized him until an Illinois acquaintance, Congressman E. B. Washburne, waiting as a one-man reception committee, stepped forth from the early-morning gloom.

2

LINCOLN rode with Washburne, in the latter's carriage, to Willard's Hotel. This massive building, six stories high, a hundred yards square, was already busy as a hive and was to grow even busier

* Superior figures refer to the section of Notes at the end of the book.

with the arrival of the President-elect. Set aside for him was a large second-floor suite on the front corner overlooking Pennsylvania Avenue and, at a little distance, a part of the White House grounds. As a center of political activity, Willard's Hotel was to eclipse the nearby White House for the next ten days.

Waiting for Lincoln, at the hotel, was William H. Seward. Most of the time Seward had a cigar in his hand or in his mouth. His mouth was large and mobile; his beaklike nose also was large; indeed, his whole head, with its broad brow and silvery hair, was somewhat oversized for his slender neck and slight build. Yet, overall, his appearance gave an impression of distinction as well as oddity, of inner resources as well as a certain feebleness. His eyes were lively and aggressive. His whole expression hinted of subtlety and humor, of worldly wisdom, of eagerness to be doing and, at the same time, of a kind of weariness with everything. Here, in fact, was a man who aspired to power and to the craftiness, though not the brutality, of a Machiavellian prince.

By the standards of Seward and his friends, Seward was far better qualified for the presidency than was Lincoln. Eight years the older of the two, Seward had gone to Union College, led the New York senate, been elected governor, and sat with Henry Clay and Daniel Webster and John C. Calhoun in the United States Senate while Lincoln was irregularly attending backwoods schools in Indiana, keeping store in New Salem, attending sessions of the Illinois legislature, struggling to get ahead as a lawyer in Springfield, and serving a single, fruitless term in Congress. During the 1850's Seward had stood out as the leader of the free-soil forces throughout the North. Even after the Lincoln-Douglas debates and Lincoln's rise to national prominence, Seward had remained the foremost Republican, the one with the best prospects for the presidency—until Lincoln beat him out at the Chicago nominating convention in 1860.

Now, at Lincoln's invitation, Seward was to be secretary of state, the number-one man in the new cabinet. He did not intend to be an ordinary State Department head. Even as a senator, in 1849–1850, he had dominated one administration, that of the rough soldier Zachary Taylor. As a cabinet chief, from March 4, 1861, he could expect to control at least as easily the administration of Abraham Lincoln, whose potentialities he as yet recognized no better than most of his contemporaries did.

If Seward should get his way, the new government would deal with secession in a manner far less firm and forceful than Lincoln was thinking of. At one time Seward had spoken of an "irrepressible conflict" between the North and the South, but he no longer talked as if the conflict were irrepressible. Secession he considered a kind of insanity that was soon to pass. "The question then is, what in these times—when people are laboring under the delusion that they are going out of the Union and going to set up for themselves—ought we to do in order to hold them in?" The answer, Seward thought, was to follow the example of every good father in dealing with sulky members of his family. "That is, be patient, kind, paternal, forbearing, and wait until they come to reflect for themselves." That is, in other words, do little or nothing while allowing the Southerners time to regain their senses. Or, perhaps, bring the family quarrel quickly to an end by picking a fight with outsiders. "I am very sure that if anybody were to make a descent on New York tomorrow— whether Louis Napoleon, or the Prince of Wales, or his mother, or the Emperor of Russia, or the Emperor of Austria, all the hills of South Carolina would pour forth their population for the rescue of New York." This had drawn laughs.[2]

Signs at the moment, as Lincoln ambled wearily into Willard's Hotel, suggested that Seward with his temporizing policy was indeed to have the upper hand. Seward appeared to be calling the tune. He it was who, sending his son Frederick as a messenger to warn Lincoln, had brought the President-elect to Washington ahead of time. He it was who now played the role of host, receiving Lincoln as a guest in Lincoln's own temporary home. He it was who stood ready to conduct him about the city, which he knew so much more intimately than the newcomer, on a round of social and official visits.

After retiring to his bedroom, to rest for a couple of hours, and then eating breakfast by himself, Lincoln left with Seward to pay a courtesy call on President James Buchanan, in the White House. Buchanan, his wry neck giving a dignified tilt to his white-topped head, politely came down the stairs to greet his visitors, then took them up to meet his cabinet, whose session had been interrupted.

The Buchanan cabinet, while still made up of Democrats, was not the same as it had been a few months earlier, when secession began. At that time the leading members had been Southern secessionists; now they were gone, and their places occupied by Northern Unionists. Buchanan himself, after trying to steer between the sectional extremes, took a somewhat more positive course after gaining fresh advisers. He had told congressmen, when they met early in December, 1860, that constitutionally a state had no right to secede but, constitutionally, the Federal government had no right to use force against a state if it did secede. Yet, despite the protests of South Carolina, he refused to overrule Major Robert Anderson after the Major, on December 26, had moved his small garrison from Fort Moultrie to the more defensible Fort Sumter, in Charleston Harbor. Stiffening even more, Buchanan in January sent a chartered merchant ship, *Star of the West*, with supplies and (below deck) troops to strengthen Sumter. He neglected to inform Anderson, however, or to give him clear instructions. Buchanan took no action after the ship ran into the fire of the seceders' shore batteries and, with no encouragement from Anderson's guns at Sumter, was compelled to turn back. Buchanan shrank from the risk of war, and so did Anderson. Both men played for time, hoping to the last for compromise and continued peace.

Buchanan's policy, while not entirely the same as Seward's, had more in common with Seward's than with Lincoln's. Buchanan, like Seward, favored a waiting game. But Buchanan was on the way out, and the others on the way in. He hesitated because, among other things, he wished to defer the crisis to the Republicans, whom he considered more to blame for it than he or his party, and more responsible for its solution. Lincoln had neither Buchanan's nor Seward's reasons for a do-little or do-nothing policy. Still, as he bade Buchanan good-bye at the end of their brief visit, Lincoln could be grateful for some of the precedents that Buchanan had set. Buchanan had upheld, however feebly, the principle of the integrity and perpetuity of the Union. He had asserted, however hesitantly, the government's claim to property in the seceded states. And he had exercised, however inconclusively, the power of the government to make secure the places that its soldiers still held.

Back at Willard's, later in the day, Lincoln was re-united with his wife and his three sons, who had made the trip to Washington on the train that he, too, orig-inally had planned to take. At the station, when his fam-ily arrived, a small crowd had braved the cold rain in the hope of getting a look at the President-elect. During the afternoon, important callers appeared at the hotel. Among them were General Winfield Scott, Senator Stephen A. Douglas along with the rest of the Illinois delegation in Congress, and Francis P. Blair with his son Montgomery.

General Scott, now old and gouty and obese, could hardly get around without assistance. He had an appe-tite for fine food and wine as well as literature, not to mention fine writing of his own, adorned with classical quotations. With his pompous manner and his elegant uniform—an undress blue frock coat, with eagle-covered brass buttons and velvet collar and cuffs—he might seem to strangers like the very caricature of a military man. In truth he had been a real soldier. He fought with distinction in the War of 1812, and he led the way to victory in the Mexican War. Eventually he rose, on his merits, to the top of the army command. Though born a Southerner, in Virginia, he was governed by loyalty to his country, not to his section or his state. When South Carolina prepared to secede, he recommended that the Charleston forts be reinforced, and especially Fort Sumter, which he pointed out as the key to the harbor. He remembered that, at the time of the South Carolina nullification crisis in 1832–1833, President Andrew Jackson had sent reinforcements and had declared he was not making war on South Carolina, but if she resisted with force, she would be making war on the United States. Among the influences which, in 1860–1861, put at least a little vigor into President Buchanan's policy, the advice of General Scott was one of the most important.

Now, shaking hands with the General at Willard's, Lincoln met the man upon whose professional competence he had been depending, for months, for the holding and retaking of the Southern forts. Unfortunately for Lincoln, as he was soon enough to learn, the General by this time was in the process of changing his mind about the feasibility and desirability of reconquest or even reinforcement.

Senator Douglas still differed with Lincoln, as he had done for many years, and still greeted him, as always, with the camaraderie of an old, familiar rival in politics. Douglas, one of the three candidates whom Lincoln had defeated in the election of 1860, had to suppress his envy of the President-elect, as Seward also did. And Douglas, again like Seward, was all for humoring and appeasing the rebellious spirits of the South.

Quite different was the position of the Blairs. The old man and his two sons, Montgomery and Frank, all Democrats who had turned Republican, exerted a good deal of power in the politics of two border states, Maryland and Missouri. Once an adviser of President Jackson, the senior Blair now took it upon himself to become an adviser of President Lincoln. Already, months earlier, he had sent Lincoln a letter urging him to announce that he meant to defend the country against all conspirators. On the day of Lincoln's arrival he had come in with Montgomery, from their estate just outside the District of Columbia, at Silver Spring, to see Lincoln in person and press Montgomery's claims to a place in the cabinet.

Montgomery Blair, a tall, lean, hatchet-faced man with small and deep-set eyes, always spoke of secessionists deliberately but defiantly, though the family had many secessionist relatives. In his cold animus there was not a trace of the abolitionist spirit. True, he had won the respect of some abolitionists by serving as counsel for the slave Dred Scott, but he was no Negrophile. His racist convictions were as strong as his Unionist convictions, and these were strong indeed.

"The real cause of the trouble," he believed, "arises from the notion generally entertained at the South that the men of the North are inferiors, and the rebellion springs altogether from pride which revolts against submission to supposed inferiors. You hear these blusterers say everywhere that one Southern man is equal to half a dozen Yankees, and that feeling has impelled them to appeal from the Constitutional mode of determining who shall govern, to arms. They will not submit, they say, to mere numbers made up of the *Mudsills*, the factory people and shopkeepers of the North. They swell just like the grandiloquent Mexicans. And I really fear that nothing short of the lesson we had to give Mexico to teach the Spanish don better manners, will ever satisfy the Southern Gascons that the people of the North are their equals even upon the field upon which they have now chosen to test the question."

As Blair saw it, the way to deal with such people, the way to preserve the Union, was certainly not to cater to their fantastic self-esteem by yielding in the slightest to their demands. That would only increase the Southerners' contempt for the North; it would only lessen the chances for reunion. The thing to do was to meet the challenge and enforce the laws. War—"the application of force involving the destruction of life"—would be the quickest and most effective means of bringing the sections together again. Once the North had "vindicated the laws and secured respect even at the cost of blood," in a short time the bitterness on both sides would disappear, and the good feelings of true Unionism would return.[3]

Blair and Seward thoroughly disliked one another. Blair saw Seward as a Whig, an antislavery man, and an appeaser. Seward saw Blair as a Democrat, a pro-slavery man, and a warmonger. Seward did not mind when the Blairs, father and son, departed from the hotel. Again he had Lincoln to himself. He took him home for dinner, with the incoming vice president, Hannibal Hamlin.

When Lincoln got back to Willard's, after dinner, his long day was not yet over. He had to shake hands with a roomful of people waiting for him. At nine o'clock he received the delegates attending the peace conference in Willard's Dancing Hall, adjoining the hotel —a conference which the state of Virginia had sponsored in a last, hopeless attempt to frame an acceptable compromise. The Virginia gentleman and former president, John Tyler, headed the delegation. Present also was the former free-soil Democratic governor of Ohio, a big, statesmanlike-appearing man, Salmon P. Chase, who was to become secretary of the treasury in Lincoln's cabinet.

It was late when the last visitors finally left. For Lincoln, this Saturday, February 23, 1861, strenuous though it had been, was only the first of a long succession of weary, wearing days. Men and issues were to keep crowding in upon him, even before actual responsibility was in his grasp—men and issues constantly demanding answers, decisions. Little questions must not be allowed to get in the way of the big one, the question of basic policy and its presentation to the people. Lincoln had given a copy of his inaugural draft to Seward and another to the senior Blair. He awaited their comments.

3

ON SUNDAY, with Seward still shepherding him about, Lincoln attended church at St. Johns, and on Monday, again with Seward, he visited the Senate, the House of Representatives, and the Supreme Court. During the rest of the week he spent most of his time in the big, crowded parlor of the hotel suite. From early in the morning till late at night he faced politicians, newspapermen, well-wishers, self-appointed advisers, and jobseekers, always jobseekers. As if he had nothing better to do than to divide the spoils of office! Yet the patronage was no mere irrelevancy, no mere intrusion upon his time. The strength of his party and his administration, even the future of his country, might well depend upon the nature of his appointments, low as well as high. Every office, from postmastership to cabinet post, needed to be filled by the man whose appointment would do the most to overcome personal, factional, partisan, and sectional strains. Seward and others urged Lincoln to name Southerners for important places in the new government and, meanwhile, to remove no one from Federal office in the state of Virginia.

Virginia, Virginia—the key to continued peace and ultimate reunion, as Lincoln again and again was told. By his forbearance with the patronage there, he could presumably help to appease the Virginians and keep the state from seceding. But he must do more than that, Seward believed. Already Seward had reminded him how "very painful" were the appeals for concession, for compromise, which came from the Union men of the border and the Upper South. "They say that without it their states all go with the tide, and your Administration must begin with the free states meeting all Southern states in a hostile Confederacy." If Virginia should go, so probably would the others.

The Virginians were divided among themselves. A few of them, and only a very few, were thoroughgoing Unionists, men who considered secession neither a constitutional right nor a sensible course. The rest, the great majority, could be classified as either moderate or extreme secessionists. The moderates recommended waiting until the new President should have demonstrated his policy with regard to coercion or compromise. And most of the moderates would be satisfied with no compromise short of the following: First, the Northern states must repeal their personal-liberty laws, that is, their laws hindering the capture and return of fugitive slaves. Second, the institution of slavery must be guaranteed forever in the District of Columbia and in the states where it was already established. Third, slaveowners must be permitted to take their slave property into all, or at least the southern part, of the Western territories, and to keep such property there.\Even those terms would not have satisfied the extremists, who demanded immediate secession (and some of whom clamored for the seizure, with or without secession, of the Federal stronghold Fortress Monroe). Unionists, moderates, and extremists all agreed that if the Federal government should attempt to "coerce" the seceding states, Virginia would join them.[4]

This was no empty threat. Already a convention to consider secession was meeting in Richmond. Its more extreme members looked southward, to Charleston, South Carolina, the seedbed of secession, and to Montgomery, Alabama, the capital of the Confederacy, for inspiration and guidance. The Unionist and moderate members looked northward, to Washington, to the peace conference they had sponsored, to Seward, and ultimately to Lincoln. Upon him, upon what he did or left undone, might depend the decisive votes in the Richmond convention.

Publicly Seward had assured the Virginians, along with the rest of the wavering Southerners, that they had nothing to fear from Republican rule, that their interest in slavery would be adequately protected. Privately he corresponded and conversed with leading Unionists and moderates. These men, like Seward himself, like Lincoln too, were former Whigs. With the disappearance of the Whig party, several years earlier, they had become Democrats or Constitutional Unionists while most of their erstwhile fellow partisans in the North were becoming Republicans. Now Seward played with the idea of combining old Whigs, North and South, into a kind of peace-keeping and Union-saving coalition. When he proposed appointing Southerners to office, he had in mind Southerners of Whig background. And when he recommended Northerners, these were Whig Republicans, not former Democrats.

DETERMINATION

Seward hoped that Lincoln, once he too had talked with old Whigs from Virginia, would change his mind about concessions to the South. Seward knew only too well Lincoln's stand on compromise in recent months, when various proposals were before Congress. Lincoln had been willing to approve practically any and all proposals except the one for drawing an east-west line to separate the territories into free and slave. He said this would not settle the question but would only lead to agitation by slaveowners for acquiring new territories south of the line, in Mexico or Cuba or Central America. Having been informed of Lincoln's views, Seward in December had cast his vote against his own convictions and against the territorial compromise. Since that time, however, his Virginia friends had been impressing upon him their belief that nothing less would suffice to keep Virginia loyal. Now, Seward thought, Lincoln must yield.

Lincoln was at least willing to confer with the Virginians. One of them, after a visit at Willard's, felt confident that the new President would refrain from coercion and would insure Virginia's safety. Probably the two men had attached somewhat different meanings to the words that passed between them. Lincoln (as he had indicated not long before, in his Indianapolis speech) did not include, in his definition of "coercion," the government's holding its own forts, or retaking them, or enforcing the laws. Nor did he feel that Virginia's safety was jeopardized by anything he or his party contemplated. Apparently his visitor had not asked him to define his terms.

On another occasion, both Lincoln and his guests were more explicit. On Tuesday night, February 26, he received a group of Virginians at nine o'clock and talked with them till early the next morning. Their chief spokesman was the elderly William C. Rives, short of stature but distinguished and dignified, once the American minister to France, now a guiding spirit in the Washington peace conference. Rives hoped to dissuade Lincoln from the policy Lincoln had foreshadowed in Indianapolis. Rives and the others listened as Lincoln, sitting awkwardly, his feet on the rungs of his chair, his elbows on his bony knees, his chin on his cupped hands, related a couple of anecdotes. Growing serious, Lincoln declared that slavery must not be extended to any of the territories, and the Federal laws must be faithfully carried out. One after another, several of his visitors objected. Then Rives spoke, his voice trembling. He told Lincoln that if he used force at Fort Sumter or elsewhere in the South, Virginia would secede and he himself, old as he was, would fight for her. As one of those present remembered the scene, Lincoln straightened himself out, rose to his full height, and advanced a step toward the diminutive old man. "Mr. Rives, Mr. Rives!" he exclaimed. "If Virginia will stay in, I will withdraw the troops from Fort Sumter!"

The following day, February 27, the peace conference reconsidered a resolution, which it had voted down the day before, for recommending to Congress that the territories be divided between freedom and slavery (that the Missouri Compromise line of 1820 be revived and extended west to California). Now a number of the delegates, including all those from Illinois, changed their votes from *no* to *yes*, and the resolution passed. Around Washington the rumor ran that the President-elect had used his influence to bring about this gesture of conciliation, but the Illinois delegates insisted that they alone were responsible for their change of front. They no doubt told the truth. Certainly Lincoln did nothing to induce Congress, at this late date, to adopt the peace conference's recommendation. The conference, the hope of the Virginia Unionists and moderates, after producing a batch of futile resolutions, adjourned.

If Lincoln could and would persuade Congress and the country to accept a last-minute, all-embracing compromise, and if he could and would persuade himself to let the forts and other Federal properties and the customs collections go, perhaps he could keep Virginia perpetually in the Union. But he had no reason to believe he could keep Virginia perpetually in the Union by the mere act of giving up Fort Sumter. He seemed to consider that idea as something of a joke. Minister Schleiden, of Bremen, who had Lincoln to dinner on March 2, was informed of Lincoln's reply to Rives and the Virginians, and he retold it as evidence that the President-elect's sense of humor remained lively even in the face of national crisis. As Schleiden heard the story, the Virginians had requested Lincoln to withdraw the Sumter garrison. "Why not?" Lincoln had replied. "If you will guarantee to me the State of Virginia I shall remove the troops. A State for a fort is no bad business." Lincoln's point, it appears, was that they could *not* guarantee Virginia.[5]

4

MARCH 4, Inauguration Day, dawned with chill winds, dark clouds, and a threat of rain, though only a few drops fell. This should have been a gala occasion, and certainly there was bustle and excitement enough in the crowded streets, but there was also an air of apprehension which, far more than the lowering sky, restrained and depressed the spirits of most of the people in Washington. Many rose red-eyed and unrefreshed after a night made sleepless by the clatter of gun carriages, horses' hoofs, and militiamen's boots on the pavements. By morning, guns and guards stood ready, at strategic points in and about the city, to put down any of the uprisings or assassination attempts that were rumored and expected.

For Lincoln, too, it had been a restless night. After arising, he still pondered the note from Seward, dated two days earlier, in which Seward submitted his resignation from the cabinet. It had not turned out to be the kind of cabinet that Seward wanted. Only he himself and two others of the first six appointments were former Whigs. Chase, the secretary of the treasury, and two others were former Democrats. A Whig Republican, Henry Winter Davis, and a Democratic Republican, Montgomery Blair, both of Maryland, had been the chief competitors for the seventh and last position, that of postmaster general. Finally Lincoln had chosen Blair. Counting himself, a former Whig, Lincoln saw the completed cabinet as evenly balanced, four to four. But this was not the kind of old-Whig administration that Seward had envisaged. While disliking and disagreeing with Blair, he feared above all the influence of Chase. Now, with his resignation, he presented to Lincoln the dilemma of either losing his—Seward's—presumably indispensable advice and support or else remaking the cabinet so as to assure him the upper hand. Lincoln, however, decided to reject both alternatives. While the inaugural parade was forming in the streets, he wrote a letter asking Seward to withdraw his resignation. As Lincoln handed the letter to his private secretary to copy, he remarked: "I can't afford to let Seward take the first trick."[6]

His inaugural address was ready, the printed draft marked up with deletions and additions. Some of the changes reflected Seward's advice. The Blairs had seen nothing to add or alter, even in the most forthright passages, but Seward had wished to tone these down and to tack on a soothing peroration.

For one thing, Seward did not like the bold statement of intent to "reclaim" and to "hold, occupy and possess" the public property in the South. He thought Lincoln should speak ambiguously about using force, should hint that he might not use it at all. Earlier Lincoln's friend O. H. Browning, who saw the draft in Indianapolis, had given similar though less far-reaching advice. Browning had written:

"Would it not be judicious so to modify this as to make it read: 'All the power at my disposal will be used to hold, occupy, and possess the property and places belonging to the Government . . . ,' omitting the declara-

tion of the purpose of reclamation, which will be con-
strued into a threat or menace, and will be irritating
even in the border States? On principle the passage is
right as it now stands. The fallen places ought to be
reclaimed. But cannot that be accomplished as well or
even better without announcing the purpose in your
inaugural?"

In editing the address, Lincoln took Browning's—and
Seward's—suggestion to omit the word "reclaim," but
not Seward's further suggestion to leave out the words
"hold, occupy, and possess." Lincoln also revised the
following passage: "beyond what may be necessary for
these [that is, for holding the public property and collecting the duties] there will be no invasion of any
State." The term "State" here was unfortunate, for it
might seem to confirm the secessionist view that the
issue lay between certain states as sovereign entities, on
the one hand, and the Federal government on the other.
Lincoln rephrased the passage thus: "beyond what may
be necessary for these objects, there will be no invasion of any part of the country—no using of force
against or among the people anywhere."

For another thing, Seward did not like the concluding
line: "With *you*, and not with *me*, is the solemn question of 'Shall it be peace, or a sword?'" That was a
needlessly abrupt and challenging way to end. Seward
deleted the sentence and drafted a new paragraph,
which Lincoln rewrote and condensed, while keeping
its essential spirit: "I am loth to close . . . not enemies,
but friends . . . bonds of affection . . . mystic chords of
memory. . . ."[7]

At noon, his revised inaugural in his coat pocket,

DETERMINATION

President-elect Lincoln walked arm in arm with President Buchanan out the side door of Willard's Hotel, while a band loudly played "Hail to the Chief." In the open barouche that waited in the street, the pair sat down together. Two senators, one of them Lincoln's old friend Edward P. Baker, took the opposite seat, facing backwards. The sun shone brightly now, but the wind still blew, and the air was raw.

The presidential carriage, with prancing cavalry close around it, led off the long parade. There followed various marching bands, companies of goose-stepping militia, delegations carrying the banners of different states and territories, and straggling groups of Washingtonians. Most impressive was the huge horse-drawn float, carrying thirty-four little girls dressed in white, who represented the thirty-four states (including those of the Deep South); on each side of the float, in large letters, was the single, significant word "Union."

Along broad Pennsylvania Avenue, as the procession went by, the gusts blew dirt into the eyes of the close-packed spectators, though the entire length of the avenue had been freshly swept. From windows and balconies and housetops other people watched, some of them with hostile glares. Also watching, from flat roofs here and there, were militiamen with loaded rifles. The people with a good enough view could observe that Buchanan appeared grave and Lincoln calm, utterly impassive, his stovepipe hat in his lap, and that the two men had very little to say to one another.

Inside the north entrance to the Capitol grounds the presidential party left the carriage and walked, between two walls of stout boards, erected to foil assassins, to the

Capitol and on to the Senate chamber. (Earlier this same morning the entire building had been searched, and no trace of the rumored time-bomb found.) Later Lincoln and his escorts appeared on the temporary platform at the east front of the Capitol. Behind and above him was the unfinished, truncated dome, and near by were scaffolds and cranes in a clearing of mud and sand, dotted with wooden sheds—signs that the dome eventually would be complete. In front of him was a newly put up fence, another precautionary device, and beyond it a crowd of some thirty thousand.

While Lincoln and the others sat, Senator Baker stepped forward and said, simply: "Fellow-citizens, I introduce to you Abraham Lincoln, President-elect of the United States." The crowd cheered.

Lincoln rose. He laid his sheaf of printed and marked-up pages on the table before him and put his gold-headed cane on top of them, as a paperweight. He reached into his pocket, brought out a pair of steel-bowed spectacles, and placed them carefully and deliberately on his nose. Then he picked up the first sheet and proceeded to read, speaking in a high-pitched but clear, strong voice, which had gained practice at many an outdoor rally in Illinois.

He began by reassuring the South that "the property, peace, and security of no section" was to be "in any wise endangered by the now incoming administration." He had no intention of interfering with slavery in the slaveholding states, and he was willing to see the Constitution amended so as to guarantee the institution forever in the places where it already existed. He believed, moreover, that fugitive slaves ought to be delivered up, so long as the liberty of free Negroes was safeguarded.

Picking up one sheet after another, he went on to dispose of the constitutional argument. "The Constitution, the Union of these States, is perpetual." "The central idea of secession is the essence of anarchy." "Physically speaking, we cannot separate."

He indicated, mildly, his firm resolve. "I shall take care, as the Constitution itself expressly enjoins upon me, that the laws of the Union be faithfully executed in all the States." He would "hold, occupy, and possess. . . ."

He stated the central issue, as he saw it. "One section of our country believes slavery is right, and ought to be extended, while the other believes it is wrong, and ought not to be extended. This is the only substantial dispute."

Then he pleaded for patience. "Nothing valuable can be lost by taking time."

Finally, just before his closing appeal, he came to the question of war or peace. "In *your* hands, my dissatisfied fellow countrymen," he said, addressing the faraway Confederates, "and not in *mine,* is the momentous issue of civil war. The government will not assail *you.* You can have no conflict, without being yourselves the aggressors. *You* have no oath registered in Heaven to destroy the government, while *I* shall have the most solemn one to 'preserve, protect, and defend' it. You can forbear the *assault;* I can *not* shrink from the *defense* of it."

After he had ended, there was a burst of applause

from the audience, which had been quiet throughout his address. The withered and feeble chief justice, Roger B. Taney, got up to administer the presidential oath—Taney, the Marylander who, in the Dred Scott decision, had held that Negroes were not intended or entitled to be citizens. The big Bible was opened, and Lincoln placed one hand upon it. With firmness and conviction (no empty ritual, this) he repeated the words: "I, Abraham Lincoln, do solemnly swear that I will faithfully execute the office of President of the United States, and will, to the best of my ability, preserve, protect, and defend the Constitution of the United States." Having concluded, he bent down and kissed the Book.

Cannon fired. A band struck up. President Lincoln and ex-President Buchanan returned to their carriage. At the White House, that afternoon, Seward called. He was going to remain in the cabinet, after all. Neither in the game of patronage nor in the game of policy had he taken the first trick. Lincoln still held the high cards.[8]

2. Hesitation

1

IT was their first morning in the White House, and the President's wife and two boys, with a retinue of relatives and servants, eagerly set out on an exploring tour. From room to room they went, Willie and Tad keeping the servants busy with questions, Mrs. Lincoln surveying each scene with a view to her future role in it. Most impressive were the parlors on the ground floor, especially the largest, the East Room, where she was to preside as hostess at grand receptions, and the most ornate, the Red Room, where her husband was to entertain his friends after dinner parties. In the unflattering light of day, however, even these rooms looked less magnificent than she had expected them to look. They, like all the rest, needed new furniture, new draperies, new paint. She was disappointed, but she could soon put things aright, and she prepared to do so.[1]

That same morning, March 5, her husband was far more deeply disappointed, and he could find no such simple and direct way to straighten matters out. When he went to his office, above the East Room, he already had cares enough, but he also had at least a basic policy for dealing with his problems, and he could expect the worst of them to wait for solution at his leisure. Presumably Fort Sumter and the other three forts not yet lost, the three in Florida, would remain safely in Federal hands for an indefinite period. Presumably the United States could continue, with no special effort, to "hold, occupy, and possess" these places while Lincoln gave his attention, first, to the routine chores of staffing and organizing the new government, and then to the delicate task of recovering the properties that the Southerners had seized. So he had had reason to believe, but so he could believe no longer, in the light of what he learned after arriving at his office that morning.

On his desk lay a batch of communications from Fort Sumter—documents of "a most important and unexpected character," as Joseph Holt, the holdover war secretary from the Buchanan cabinet, said in his covering letter. During the past several weeks, Holt went on to explain, the fort's commander, Major Robert Anderson, had reported regularly the progress of the hostile batteries under construction around him in Charleston Harbor, but he never had intimated that these works compromised his safety, nor had he suggested that reinforcements or even additional supplies should be sent to him. Now, suddenly, Anderson had begun to express doubts about his ability to keep possession of Sumter. On the one hand, he stated that his stores were running low, would be exhausted in a matter of weeks. On the other hand, he gave it as his considered opinion that an effort to throw in reinforcements and supplies, so as to enable him to hold on, would require a force of not less than 20,000 "good and well disciplined men." For such an undertaking, Holt indicated in his letter to Lincoln, the War Department was quite unprepared. Holt explained that Anderson's recent declarations had taken the department by surprise.

When Lincoln read them, they took him the same way. He wondered about Anderson's loyalty. Anderson, a Kentuckian, had family connections with the Lower South. In one of his reports he had written: "I do hope that no attempt will be made by our friends to throw supplies in—their doing so would do more harm than good." Had he been scheming to delay relief and reinforcement until he would be beyond help, and the fort would have to be evacuated? In fairness to Anderson it must be said that he found himself in a torturous, exposed, ambiguous position, without clear orders from the War Department, without a sharp definition of his most unusual responsibilities. It must be added that, to the end, he was to do his duty, not uncomplainingly but on the whole faithfully, as an officer of the United States Army. In fairness to the suspicious Lincoln, however, it must also be said that, almost to the last, Anderson hoped in his heart of hearts for a peaceful separation of the country.

Shocked and dismayed, Lincoln felt the need of expert military advice. He called in his general in chief, the portly hulk of what had been the Hero of Chapultepec, Winfield Scott. He handed Scott the sheaf of papers he had been poring over. He asked him to take them along, read them, and comment upon them.

That night Lincoln got the documents back—not from Scott himself but from William H. Seward—and with them a note which Scott had appended to Holt's letter and had "respectfully submitted to the President, thro' the Secretary of State." Scott could not have submitted his reply through Lincoln's secretary of war, Simon Cameron, for Cameron had not yet arrived in Washington. He chose not to submit it through Buchanan's secretary of war, Holt, though Holt was acting in Cameron's place for the time being. He chose, instead to submit it through Lincoln's secretary of state, Seward, that man of many devices. Evidently Seward was close to Scott and, just as evidently, conceived of himself as heading more than one department if not, indeed, the whole administration.

With regard to Sumter, Scott's note was even more discouraging than Anderson's reports had been. Scott opined that, three months earlier, it would have been easy enough to reinforce the garrison, but now it would be ten or fifteen times as hard. The chance to save the fort had passed. "I now see no alternative but a surrender, in some weeks," Scott advised. "Evacuation seems almost inevitable, & in this view our distinguished Chief Engineer (Brigadier Totten) concurs—if, indeed, the worn out garrison be not assaulted & carried in the present week." Surrender in a few days or, at most, a few weeks! So much for the prospects of holding Fort Sumter.

And, as Lincoln gathered from Scott's note, this was not the only fort in jeopardy. There was also Fort Pickens, off Pensacola, in Florida. The Pickens situation in some respects paralleled the Sumter one. Pickens, like Sumter, sat upon an island in the harbor, and the Federal garrison (on January 10) had moved into it from a more vulnerable position (Fort Barrancas) on the mainland. As in Charleston Harbor, so too in Pensacola Harbor the rebels seized various strongholds, including in this case a navy yard, and began to build these up so as to threaten the one point that Union troops still occupied. To be made secure, Fort Pickens should be reinforced, but it could not be reinforced without a certain embarrassment. Some kind of "truce or informal understanding," as Scott now intimated to Lincoln, stood in the way.

In fact, a gentlemen's agreement had been concluded between the Buchanan administration and the Florida authorities at the end of January. The circumstances were these: the Buchanan administration had sent the *Brooklyn* and other warships with men and provisions for Fort Pickens, and the Floridians had prepared to forestall the expedition by assaulting the fort. The terms of the agreement, which at the last minute had averted a clash, were the following: the state batteries would withhold their fire, and the Union squadron would land the provisions but not the men, who were to remain on board the *Brooklyn*. At any time, however, the men would be landed if the fort should be attacked "or preparations made for its attack." Since the end of January the truce had grown more and more precarious, with the Floridians working feverishly to bring additional firepower to bear on Pickens, and with the Federal ships hovering ominously offshore.

All together, the information and advice which Lincoln received on his first full day in office were enough to stagger a less determined or less resilient man. He paused, but he did not reel. He refused to accept, without further inquiry, the opinion of his military experts, weighty though their authority was. Before going to bed that night, he decided he would direct General Scott to undertake a thorough investigation of the Sumter problem. Meanwhile, he would tell the general to exercise full vigilance for the maintenance of all places belonging to the United States.[2]

2

THE next day, Wednesday, the top men of the War and Navy departments conferred among themselves with regard to the practicability of reinforcing Sumter. That night, at his first cabinet meeting, Lincoln said nothing about the subject. Indeed, he brought up no business at all, his only purpose being to formalize the beginning of his administration and to introduce the members, in their new capacities, to one another.

There they sat around a table in the order of the seniority of their positions. Seward, with his big head thrust forward and a knowing expression on his world-weary face. Salmon P. Chase, secretary of the treasury, with a drooping eyelid and an air of being conscious that he was in fact as much the statesman as he appeared to be. (Simon Cameron, secretary of war, a thin-lipped, canny Scot—not yet present.) Edward Bates, attorney general, a plain, thick-set, bewhiskered man, once the owner of slaves. Montgomery Blair, postmaster general, cautious and slow of speech, grim, with a face the least bit like a rodent's. Gideon Welles, secretary of the navy, who wore a huge gray wig and a long gray beard and who, but for his spectacles, would almost have resembled Neptune. Caleb B. Smith, secretary of the interior, with a neat appearance, a smooth manner, a habit of conservative, conformist thinking, and a lisp.

On Thursday, Lincoln met in his office with Scott, Holt, Welles, and a few other military and naval men. On Friday night, in the East Room, he and Mrs. Lincoln held their first reception—"a motley crowd and a terrible squeeze," it seemed to the diary-keeping Bates. All along there was for Lincoln the pressure of social obligations as well as patronage demands, in addition to the strain of policy decisions.

On Saturday night he faced his cabinet counselors again, and this time he told them what was on his mind. Fort Sumter, according to the highest military authorities, must be abandoned. The place had provisions enough to last for no more than twenty-eight days. If it were to be held, it would have to be relieved within that time, but this would require a force of 20,000 men, and these could not be raised soon enough. Even if, somehow, they could be raised, the attempt to use them would probably lead to a sanguinary battle.

Most of the cabinet members were astonished at this news, as Bates confessed he was. Blair was disgusted as well. But Seward was neither surprised nor displeased. Nor did he see any reason to object when the others agreed that the President should seek more detailed and more precise information. So Lincoln wrote out three questions for the General in Chief—questions he had asked before and now repeated with insistence: How long, at the most, could the Sumter garrison hold on? Could it be either reinforced or provisioned with the forces already available? If not, what additional forces would be needed?

Meanwhile, Lincoln hoped to act, to do something, however small, that might help to head off the secessionists. They appeared to be arming themselves fast. At least, perhaps, he could stop the flow of arms and ammunition from the North to the South. Unfortunately, as the acting head of the War Department wrote in response to a presidential inquiry, "under existing laws, the Department has no power—nor has the government any—to prevent the shipment of munitions of war to the seceding States."

On Monday, one week after the inauguration, came Scott's replies to Lincoln's written queries. To "supply and re-enforce" Sumter, the General now said, he would have to have a fleet of warships and transports which, with the navy scattered as it was, could not be got together in less than four months. He would also need 5,000 regular troops and 20,000 volunteers; raising and training these men would require from six to eight months. Without such an armada and such an army he could not hope to take Fort Moultrie and the other batteries inside and outside Charleston Harbor, and without first taking all these he could not hope to succeed at Sumter. "As a practical military question," the old veteran concluded, "the time for succoring Sumter with any means at hand had passed away nearly a month ago. Since then a surrender under assault or from starvation has been merely a question of time."

Scott considered the matter as settled. Indeed, he already had drafted the "*projet* of a letter" that he desired authorization for sending to Major Anderson: ". . . you will, after communicating your purpose to His Excellency, the Governor of South Carolina, engage suitable water transportation, & peacefully evacuate Fort Sumter. . . ."

Lincoln was far from being ready to approve any such order. He could not see how he was going to do anything to make it possible for the garrison to hold on. Still, at the very least, he could reassert his basic intention, and this he did. On the same day he heard from Scott, he sent to him the message he had given orally almost a week before and had asked his private secretary, John G. Nicolay, to put in writing two days before. "I am directed by the President," Nicolay had written, "to say he desires you to exercise all possible vigilance for the maintenance of all the places within the military department of the United States."

So far as Fort Pickens was concerned, Lincoln could do more than that. He could, and did, take a specific, positive step. He now directed Scott to send orders, to the officer in command of the troops on board the *Brooklyn,* for landing the troops at the first favorable moment, reinforcing the fort, and holding it at any cost.[3]

3

DURING that first week of the new administration, from March 5 to March 11, while the President strove, despite obstacles, to "hold, occupy, and possess" the forts, the Secretary of State moved, on his own initiative, in quite the opposite direction. Seward, the man officially in charge of foreign affairs, viewed disunion as a problem in diplomacy. It was a question of the relationship of the Federal government to other power centers—in Europe, in the Confederacy, and in Virginia and other undecided states of the border and the Upper South. The Seward policy aimed to reunite the country by talking loud to foreigners and soft to doubtful or disaffected Americans. For the time being, so far as Seward saw, Europe presented no urgent occasion for the use of diplomatic talent, but the Confederacy and even more the border states seemed to him to necessitate quick appeasement.

Throughout the South the President's inaugural address had antagonized secessionists and disheartened their opponents. The excitable *Richmond Enquirer* called it a war declaration: "Sectional war, declared by Mr. Lincoln, awaits only the signal gun from the insulted Southern Confederacy, to light its horrid fires all along the border of Virginia. No action of our Convention can now maintain the peace. *She must fight!* The liberty of choice is yet hers. She may march to the contest with her sister States of the South, or she *must* march to the conflict *against* them. There is left no middle course; there is left no more peace; war must settle the conflict, and the God of battle give victory to the right!" A leading Virginia Unionist confessed that the inaugural had "had a most unhappy influence upon some of the members of our convention." Apparently the chances were that the convention might vote, any day now, to remove the state from the Union.

Seward took prompt steps to reassure the Virginians. He asked one of the editors of the *National Intelligencer*, the most respected newspaper in Washington, to go to Richmond and tell the leader of the Unionists in the state convention, George W. Summers, that the new administration would make no attempt to strengthen or hold Fort Sumter. Then Seward dashed off a note to Lincoln. "What do you think of *George W. Summers* for Justice of Supreme Court," he wrote. "It would totally demoralize disunion in the Border States." (The Governor of Maryland agreed in principle, only his preferred candidate for the court vacancy was Senator John J. Crittenden, of Kentucky. "If . . . he or some such man shall be appointed by you," the Governor advised Lincoln, "it would be hailed by the unionists throughout the South, and everywhere, as a practical interpretation of the declaration that your Inaugural meant peace.")

Seward also took steps to mollify the Confederates. Representing the Confederacy, in Washington, were three commissioners—ambassadors to what they considered a foreign government. They had instructions to negotiate for the transfer of forts from the United States to the Confederate States. Through a succession of go-betweens they kept in touch with Seward.

The first of the commissioners' agents heard from Seward, and reported directly to the Montgomery government, that Lincoln did not really mean what he appeared to mean in his inaugural address. Seward explained that, when Lincoln referred to the collection of the revenues, "he had an eye more to the ports outside than inside the Confederates States . . . that New York and San Francisco might at any time . . . refuse to pay over the customs"! As for Lincoln's words "hold, occupy, and possess," these were intended to be taken with the phrases that followed and qualified them, that is, the phrases "so far as practicable, unless my rightful masters the American people shall withhold the requisite means, or in some authoritative manner direct the contrary." These phrases—so Seward insisted—implied that the question of the forts was to be submitted to the people in some appropriate manner (perhaps through a referendum, perhaps through a specially called national convention). All this the Confederates took with the skepticism it deserved.

The commissioners were impatient to gain a hearing and to get on with their negotiations. At first Seward promised to let them know how best to bring the subject of their mission before the President and the cabinet. Then he began to stall them off by saying the administration did not yet have time to deal properly with a matter so important. The President, he explained, was "besieged" by applicants for office and was "surrounded by all the difficulties and confusion incident to the first days of a new administration." Seward gave the commissioners to understand, however, that Sumter very soon would be evacuated anyhow. When they demanded an informal conference with him (at no time had they and he met face to face) he said he would have to consult the President. The answer he later relayed back to them was No, it would not be in his power to receive the gentlemen.

The rumors which Seward had started, about the early abandonment of Sumter, eventually appeared in the press. They made "great news" in the metropolitan dailies on Monday, March 11, the very day on which Lincoln, in his orders to Scott, reaffirmed the opposite policy—a fact which the newspapers did not report and did not know.

As the news spread, it had, on the whole, a calming effect in Richmond and elsewhere in the non-Confederate South. "The removal from Sumter," said George W. Summers, writing on behalf of the Virginia Unionists, and writing as if the removal already were a fact, "acted like a charm—it gave us great strength. A reaction is now going on in the State."

In Washington, the Confederate commissioners agreed to postpone their demand for an immediate reception. They would wait, but only for a couple of weeks, until about March 28, and only on condition that the existing military status of the Union forts remain absolutely unchanged.

In Charleston, the publishers and the readers of the *Mercury* and the *Courier* rejoiced that Sumter would soon fall without a fight. The harbor itself grew relatively quiet. "The news . . . seems to have caused an almost entire cessation of work on the batteries around us," one of Anderson's officers wrote to the War Department from the fort. "Unless otherwise directed I shall discharge my force when the orders for evacuation arrive. . . ."

In the city of New York—and throughout the free states of the North—there was a mixed reaction to the news. "Some say it will break the neck of 'secession' in South Carolina itself, and ruin every secessionist leader," a New Yorker recorded. "Some say the talk of evacuating Fort Sumter is a ruse to disarm South Carolina and facilitate the introduction of reinforcements." Some thought the decision unfortunate but unavoidable. Some, especially Buchanan Democrats and also businessmen with Southern connections, heartily approved. And some, particularly the radical Republicans for whom Horace Greeley's *New York Tribune* spoke, were incensed.[4]

4

THE BLAIRS were much distressed by General Scott's evacuation proposal and by the rumor that Sumter was indeed to be sacrificed. Equally distressed were most of the Republicans in the Senate, which continued in executive session (mainly to pass upon the new President's appointments). The elder Blair, induced as he said by "some of our friends in the Senate & out of it," called at the White House to register his, and their, protest. He told Lincoln that a withdrawal from the fort would be a "surrender of the Union" unless the withdrawal were made "under irresistible force." Blair thought Lincoln should issue a proclamation denouncing treason and asserting an intent to enforce the laws—the kind of proclamation that President Jackson had issued some thirty years before, when South Carolina attempted to "nullify" the tariff acts.

The next morning, March 13, Blair's son Montgomery, the grimly determined postmaster general, hurried to the White House with a brother-in-law, Gustavus Vasa Fox. This man, too, had an air of urgency and determination, along with a strong chin, a bald dome, energetic gestures, and a habit of systematic thought. Now thirty-nine, Fox had graduated from Annapolis and served for many years as a naval officer (he supervised the transport of troops to Vera Cruz during the Mexican War) before retiring and entering the textile business in Massachusetts. Recently he had been studying the Sumter situation, and he had come to conclusions quite different from those of Scott. Relief could be got to the fort, Fox believed, not in six or eight months but in a matter of days, certainly in plenty of time to save the garrison. He was sure the tactical problems could be solved, though he recognized that they would be difficult.

Fort Sumter, of course, had not been designed to meet the dangers that now threatened it. It had been designed to guard Charleston's inner harbor, in co-operation with other works, against a hostile force approaching the city from the sea. The fort, with brick and concrete walls sixty feet high and eight to twelve feet thick, stood on a tiny artificial island, made of refuse granite brought down from Northern quarries. The site, more than three miles from Charleston itself, was just within the harbor entrance, between two points of land—Sullivan's Island on the north and Morris Island on the south—but closer to the southern one. A pentagon, the fort pointed northward toward the ship channel and exposed a flat side, with unprotected docks and sally ports, toward the nearest land, in the rear. The fort was still under construction (the workmen as well as the soldiers had to be fed) and only about half of its guns had yet been mounted.

The other harbor fortifications were now in hostile hands. These works surrounded Sumter. They included Fort Johnson, Castle Pinckney, Fort Moultrie, the battery at Cummings Point, other gun emplacements on Morris Island, and a "floating battery" which the Confederates were preparing and which they could anchor close to Sumter's weakest side. From Moultrie (on Sullivan's Island) to Sumter, the distance was only a mile and an eighth, and from Cummings Point (on Morris Island) only three-quarters of a mile.

Any expedition to relieve Sumter would have to pass between the Scylla of Fort Moultrie and the Charybdis of Cummings Point, unless the expedition should first silence the guns of one or both. Even before reaching the harbor mouth, however, the relief ships could

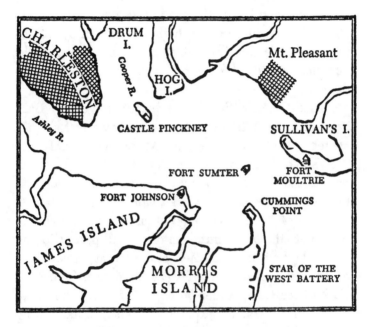

Charleston Harbor. From John G. Nicolay,
The Outbreak of the Rebellion (New York:
Scribner, 1881).

be expected to run into serious opposition—as, indeed, the *Star of the West* had done when, in January, the Buchanan administration sent it with supplies and men. Across the outer harbor, four miles away from Sumter, lay a long sand bar. Only small vessels of shallow draft could get past this, even at high tide, except by way of the man-made channels, which the Confederates could obstruct, if indeed they had not already obstructed them.

Fox, the man with a plan whom Montgomery Blair brought to the White House, was well aware of all this. So, too, were General Scott and Major Anderson. Hence Scott's and Anderson's conviction that a very large expedition, one strong enough to force an entrance and take all the Confederate works, would be necessary. At the time of Lincoln's inauguration, Anderson had not ruled out "the little stratagem of a small party slipping in," and a few small steamers of the Coast Survey were all ready to set out, at a few hours' notice, from New York. Since then, Anderson as well as Scott had concluded that such an expedition could do no lasting good and might do irreparable harm. What other way could Lincoln find to relieve the fort? Through the mails he received all kinds of suggestions. One correspondent proposed that he get submarines to carry in reinforcements; another, that he use balloons to drop supplies. Still another offered to do the job himself, to outfit his own expedition and guarantee to hold Sumter a whole year—for five million dollars! By the time he met Blair's brother-in-law, Lincoln was desperate for a practicable plan.

Fox's scheme, as Fox first outlined it to Lincoln, seemed to have possibilities though also flaws. Fox said the "skillful officers at Charleston" would anticipate an effort to send boats or small steamers, incapable of bearing heavy armament, over the outer bar at high water. Those officers would have armed every steamer they could find and, at the bar, would throw their fleet at the relief vessels. Thus the Confederates would jeopardize the movement at the outset. "To elude their vigilance or attempt a stratagem however ingenious," Fox said, "I consider too liable to failure."

Instead, Fox proposed a head-on approach. He would put troops on a large transport, and supplies on two rented New York tug boats. He would convoy these by means of the heavily gunned warship *Pawnee* and the agile revenue cutter *Harriet Lane* (the only suitable craft to be had within a reasonable time). Having arrived off Charleston Harbor, he would feint a movement in order to test the intentions of the Confederates. If they undertook to oppose his entrance, he would bring the *Pawnee* and the *Harriet Lane* up to the bar and, by the use of their powerful guns, together with Fort Sumter's, he would disperse the Confederate vessels or drive them on shore. The way thus cleared, he would wait till nightfall and then, in the dark, with the troops as well as the supplies aboard the two tugs, he would run them between Fort Moultrie and Cummings Point to the relief of Anderson's beleaguered garrison.

Well and good! But even if the plan should work as Fox predicted, it obviously would do so only at the cost of much shooting and, very likely, much killing. Possibly the second stage of his tactics could be tried without the first stage, that is, the running in of tugs (or small boats) without the previous blasting of the Confederates' naval force.

About the time of his initial interview with Fox, Lincoln paid a visit to Mrs. Abner Doubleday, who was then in Washington. Her husband, an officer on Anderson's staff (and long afterwards remembered as the inventor of baseball), strongly disagreed with Anderson about the necessity and desirability of abandoning the fort. Lincoln asked Mrs. Doubleday if he might look at her husband's letters so as to get a better understanding of the Sumter situation. In one of the letters Doubleday had written that it was very hard for a gun on land to hit a small boat dancing on the waves in the daytime, and almost impossible at night, and that the garrison might therefore be reinforced and supplied by a number of small boats operating from offshore vessels as a base. Doubleday said nothing about a naval battle as a prerequisite for this.

Neither did Lincoln when, on March 14, he presented the Fox plan to his cabinet. The cabinet met twice that day, to discuss, and to hear military and naval experts discuss, the revised plan's feasibility. "The *army* officers and *navy* officers differ widely about the degree of danger to rapidly moving vessels passing under the fire of land batteries," Attorney General Bates noted. "The *army* officers think destruction almost inevitable, where the *navy* officers think the danger but slight. . . . They say the greatest danger will be in landing at Sumter, upon which point there may be a concentrated fire."

Assuming that the scheme was tactically sound—and Lincoln was willing to take his chances on that—there remained the question whether it was politically wise. There were considerations such as those a Boston friend of Seward's had put down in a letter which Seward had forwarded to Lincoln. "The object of the Secessionists is to make the United States Government the aggressor, so that if Civil War ensues, it may not be charged on them," this letter said. "They have already been disappointed that they have no act of the Government of which they can really complain, or upon which they can rouse the people of the border States to join them. They are looking to Fort Sumpter [*sic*] for such an act. They do not wish to attack it first—but if they could, by their batteries, intercept a reinforcement of supplies, and thereby call out a response from the guns of Major Anderson, they would have what *they* would call an affirmative act of aggression on the part of the United States, and would so make their people believe."

In view of these considerations, and in view of Lincoln's own inaugural statement that the secessionists could have no war without being themselves the aggressors, it was imperative for Lincoln to proceed most carefully in planning any Sumter expedition. Perhaps there was a useful hint or clue for him in another piece of mail, a letter addressed to him from J. Watson Webb, the well-known editor of the *New York Courier and Enquirer*.

"Would you evacuate Fort Sumpter," Webb asked, "if it can be provisioned and reinforced without great loss of life? I think not; and, therefore, attend upon the following suggestions. . . ." The essence of Webb's advice, though he expressed it in hurried and confused language, was this: Charter three steamers and dispatch them to provision the fort. "Do this publicly and let the destination and purpose of the expedition be proclaimed." But have the stores put into only two of the three ships, and send troops also, *"every man below."* Let the "empty or decoy Steamer" approach Charleston Harbor at least a mile ahead of the other two, to draw the Confederate fire. "The fire having been thus opened by the Rebels upon Government vessels, nobody will censure Major Anderson or the Government, if he promptly, as he can, destroys *Moultrie* and the Battery on Morris Island." The two ships with the troops and stores could then steam safely in. Of course, appropriate orders would have to be given to Anderson in advance. And remember: "Secrecy is everything to insure success. . . ."

For all its crudities, that stratagem might contain some useful features. Why not send provisions, and why not do this openly, letting the South and indeed the whole world know? Why not send provisions alone —mere food for hungry men? Surely this could not be viewed as an aggressive act, no matter what might ensue. All previous discussions of Sumter, within the administration, had linked provisioning with reinforcing, had been concerned with the sending of both supplies and troops. But a halfway measure was certainly possible, and perhaps advisable.

On March 15, Lincoln directed his private secretary to send to each of the cabinet members a note requesting a written answer to the following question: "Assuming it to be possible to now provision Fort-Sumpter [*sic*], under all the circumstances, is it wise to attempt it?"[5]

5

IT was quite wintry for March 18 in Washington, very cold and blustery, with a low, gray sky that was beginning to spit snow. Two weeks had passed since the day Lincoln learned of Sumter's predicament, two weeks during which the garrison's limited stores had been further used up. And the solution to his problem seemed at least as remote now as it had seemed then.

Another meeting of the cabinet had adjourned, and Lincoln sat alone in the cabinet room with the members' replies to his query of March 15 on the table before him. Would it be wise to undertake a provisioning of the fort?

Blair: Yes. Provision—and reinforce as well! No matter if the effort fails. "It will in any event vindicate . . . the determination of the people and their President to maintain the authority of the Government, and this is all that is wanting, in my opinion, to restore it."

Chase: Yes. In attempting to provision, the government will be exercising a "clear right" and performing a "plain duty." The action probably will not lead to war, "especially if accompanied or immediately followed by a Proclamation setting forth a liberal & generous yet firm policy toward the disaffected States."

Smith: Yes and No. On the one hand, the attempt would "doubtless induce an attack," lead to the "early loss of the fort," and eventuate in the "calamity" of civil war, which ought to be avoided at almost any cost. "If"—on the other hand—"such a conflict should become inevitable, it is much better that it should commence by the resistance of the authorities or the people of South Carolina to the legal action of the government in enforcing the laws of the United States."

Seward: No. The border states "desire to be loyal." They are "temporarily demoralized" by a sympathy for the seceded South. They are "apprehending that the Federal government will resort to military coercion," and "even though such coercion should be necessary to maintain the authority, or even the integrity, of the Union," the effect will be to precipitate the secession of the remaining slave states. "It seems to me that we will have inaugurated a civil war by our own act, without an adequate object, after which reunion will be hopeless."

Welles: No. There is only one way to keep the "armed boats of the enemy" from capturing the Sumter-bound tugs, and that is by opening fire from the fort or the ships, or both. "If this is done, will it not be claimed that aggressive war has been commenced by us upon the State and its citizens in their own harbor?" Besides, the Northern people already have been given the impression that Sumter is to be evacuated. "The public mind is becoming tranquilized under it and will become fully reconciled to it when the causes which have led to that necessity have been made public and are rightly understood."

Bates: No. "I am most unwilling to strike—I will not say the first blow, for South Carolina has already struck that—but I am unwilling *'under all the circumstances'* at this moment to do any act which may have the semblance, before the world, of beginning a civil war, the terrible consequences of which would, I think, find no parallel in modern times." Wait. Be patient. "In several of the misguided States of the South, a large portion of the people are really lovers of the Union, and anxious to be safely back, under the protection of its flag." Give those people time, and "the nation will be restored to its integrity without the effusion of blood." Let Sumter go, but strengthen and hold tight to Pickens and the rest of the Florida forts.

Cameron: No. Even if provisioned, Sumter cannot be maintained against the hostile troops and fortifications surrounding it. Take Scott's advice.

Thus the cabinet vote was four to three against provisioning, if the ambiguous Smith be counted with the affirmative, or five to two if he be numbered with the negative.

Lincoln looked up as a visitor burst into the cabinet room. It was the elder Blair again. His son Montgomery was threatening to quit the cabinet if nothing were done, and done soon, to help the Sumter garrison. "Will you give up the fort?" the old man now demanded. Avoiding a direct reply, Loncoln wearily said that most of his advisers recommended giving it up.

"It would be treason," the old man muttered as he left.

Later that day, in his office, Lincoln continued to weigh the pros and cons. Outside, the snow was coming down thickly now. What should his decision be? Should he merely count the arguments for and against, or also weigh them, and if so, how?

Viewed simply as a question of expediency—and quite apart from principle, that is, the presidential oath and the constitutional duty to enforce the laws—there seemed to be fewer arguments for trying to hold Sumter than for letting it go. In favor of making the attempt there were only two: First, it was a political necessity, for otherwise the die-hard Republicans would desert the administration, and the party would fall to pieces. Second, it was a psychological necessity, for otherwise the Confederates would claim a victory, and this would invigorate their cause.

On the other side could be listed several points: To hold Sumter very long was hardly possible, in any event. There was always the risk of a "bloody conflict." The Confederates would gain a "moral advantage" from a successful attack. Even without an attack, there was the humiliating possibility that the garrison, if not withdrawn, might have to surrender to keep from starving. Forbearance would win over the border and the Upper South and, possibly, win back the seceded states. Partisan advantage would be gained by confounding and embarrassing those Northern opponents who "have relied on the cry of 'Coercion' as a means of keeping up the excitement against the Republican Party." Anyhow, "the Fort in the present condition of affairs is of inconsiderable military value," and every strategic purpose which it could serve "would be better subserved by Ships of War, outside the Harbor."

This last suggestion, in one form or another, had come to Lincoln from various sources, including men who could claim to speak for the Upper South. For instance, Seward's friend John A. Gilmer, a Unionist congressman from North Carolina, had counseled that Lincoln ought to abandon Sumter (and the other disputed places) and content himself with collecting the customs due at Charleston (and elsewhere) on shipboard. But this advice, like all advice that Lincoln got, was controverted. A Virginia Unionist warned that South Carolina would "seize the slightest pretext for a collision" and urged that Lincoln "refrain from any effort to reinforce the forts or to collect the revenue in the seceded States."

Still, a floating customs house off Charleston ought to be less provocative than an expedition with supplies for Sumter. The one might be considered if the other had to be ruled out. So Lincoln took up his pen and composed three notes. The note to the Attorney General asked his opinion of the constitutionality and legality of collecting duties "on ship-board, off-shore" and of preventing "the landing of dutiable goods, unless the duties were paid." The note to the Secretary of the Navy asked the amount of naval force that, immediately or later on, could be "placed at the disposal of the Revenue Service." And the note to the Secretary of the Treasury asked about the general advisability of the project.

Again, Lincoln was to be frustrated. The answers he was to receive were, on the whole, discouraging.

Through his office window he could see, not far to the south, the unfinished monument to George Washington—an ugly stump of stonework, its outline now blurred and softened by the snow-filled air. That truncated obelisk could be viewed as the symbol of a nation not yet made whole.[6]

3. Decision

1

DURING the next several days, while still hesitating, Lincoln undertook to test some of the assumptions on which his advisers had based their advice. Was it, after all, impossible to provide relief for Sumter without grave risks of both bloodshed and failure? Was it really probable that, as Bates and Seward argued, a retreat from Sumter would bring about an upsurge of Unionist feeling, a rebellion against the rebellion, throughout the South?

To learn more about the practicability of a provisioning expedition, Montgomery Blair proposed that his brother-in-law Fox make an on-the-spot investigation, and Lincoln told Fox to go ahead. "Our Uncle Abe Lincoln has taken a high esteem for me," Fox wrote to his wife, "and wishes me to take dispatches to Major Anderson at Fort Sumpter with regard to its final evacuation and to obtain a clear statement of his condition which his letters, probably guarded, do not fully exhibit." Fox thought it advisable thus to mislead his wife about the impending "final evacuation," lest his true mission leak out through some tampering with his mail or through some indiscretion on her part.

Fox returned to Washington and reported to Lincoln on March 25. He had reached the fort after dark four days earlier, he said, and had remained there two hours. Anderson told him that an entrance from the sea was out of the question. "But as we looked out upon the water from the parapet," Fox now said, "it seemed very feasible, more especially as we heard the oars of a boat near the fort, which the sentries hailed, but we could not see her through the darkness until she almost touched the landing." Anderson informed him that the provisions on hand might be stretched, but only by putting the men on short rations. "I made no arrangements with Major Anderson for reenforcing or supplying the fort, nor did I inform him of my plan."

During the next few days Fox talked frequently with Blair as well as Lincoln. "Blair is nearly run to death with office seekers," he wrote to his wife. "The President is equally beset. I have seen Abe often, also Mrs. L. She is Lady Like, converses easily, dresses well and has the Kentucky pronunciation like old Mrs. Blair," that is, like Mrs. Fox's mother.

Meanwhile, to find out more about Southern Unionism, Lincoln sent another mission to Charleston. The man he chose for this, Stephen S. Hurlbut, seemed well suited for the job. Hurlbut was an old Illinois friend of Lincoln's, but he had been born and educated in Charleston, and he still had friends and relatives there. On March 21 he happened to be in Washington, and Lincoln called him to the White House. Lincoln said to him: Seward maintains that Unionism is potentially strong in the South, even in the state of South Carolina

itself. Go and see. Hurlbut agreed to go, and with him
went another of Lincoln's old Illinois acquaintances,
Ward H. Lamon (the man who had served as Lincoln's
bodyguard on that unscheduled February train ride
to Washington).

Hurlbut and Lamon spent two days in Charleston,
Hurlbut staying at his sister's home, Lamon at a hotel.
Hurlbut visited a number of his former friends and
neighbors. Taking Lamon surreptitiously along, he
talked for more than two hours with James. L. Petigru,
under whom he once had studied law. Petigru was a
witty and likeable old man, as well as a distinguished
one. At the time South Carolina seceded he had been
quoted as saying that the state was too small for a
nation and too large for an insane asylum. After leaving Petigru, Hurlbut and Lamon separated again, so
as to avoid arousing the suspicion that Hurlbut was
Lincoln's agent. Lamon attracted much the more public
attention. He made a trip to Fort Sumter and gave
Anderson to believe that the fort was about to be
abandoned. He saw the governor of South Carolina,
Francis W. Pickens, and told him the same thing. Actually, Lamon was acting more as Seward's agent than as
Lincoln's. Before departing from Charleston he wrote
to Seward that he was "satisfied of the policy and
propriety of immediately evacuating Fort Sumter."

Back in Washington, on March 27, Hurlbut filled
sixteen foolscap pages with his report to the President.
There is, he said, "no attachment to the Union" among
the Carolinians. The Stars and Stripes are nowhere to
be seen, except at Sumter. Petigru is the only Unionist

left in Charleston. Unionism appears to be almost as dead elsewhere in the South. "I solemnly believe that the Seven States are irrevocably gone—except perhaps Texas and Louisiana, as to which I have no information." So much for that. But Hurlbut also put into his report many other observations that might provide food for thought:

Item. "I learned from one of the Pilots, an acquaintance in former years, that the vessels sunk to obstruct the Ship Channel had not had that effect but had been swept out by the force of the current, making but a slight alteration on the bar."

Item. "I have no doubt that a ship known to contain *only provisions* for Sumpter would be stopped & refused admittance. Even the moderate men who desire not to open fire, [who] believe in the safer policy of time and starvation"—even these men would approve firing upon a provisioning expedition if one were sent.

Item. If Sumter is abandoned, "undoubtedly this will be followed by a demand for Pickens and the Keys of the Gulf," that is, Pickens and the other two forts in Florida.

Item. "It is my deliberate judgment, from long acquaintance with the people and the country of So. Carolina and . . . in a modified form with the other seceding States, that the attempt to fulfill the duties of the Executive Office in enforcing the laws & authority of the U. S. within their limits will be War, in fact, War in which the seceding States will be united and the others disunited."

On the day he received that report, Lincoln also had

other things to occupy his time, among them the duty of greeting a foreign ambassador, the Chevalier Bertinatti. Dressed in all his finery, the Chevalier arrived at the White House with Secretary of State Seward, his son, Fred Seward, and the London *Times* correspondent, William H. Russell. Soon there entered, as Russell viewed him, a tall, lank, lean man with a shambling, loose gait and with long pendulous arms, a man dressed in an ill-fitting, wrinkled black suit and a shirt with a turned-down collar that revealed a sinewy, muscular yellow neck. "As he advanced through the room," Russell afterwards wrote, "he evidently controlled a desire to shake hands all round with everybody, and smiled good-humouredly till he was suddenly brought up by the staid deportment of Mr. Seward, and by the profound diplomatic bows of the Chevalier Bertinatti." Russell had no understanding of the weight that then lay on Lincoln's mind and spirit.[1]

2

TIME was running out at Sumter. Lincoln could not postpone his decision much longer, and the developments of March 28 suddenly brought him to the point of making up his mind.

That morning the *New York Tribune* came out with the sensational news that, two or three weeks earlier, the administration had disregarded the truce at Pensacola and had ordered the warship *Brooklyn* to land her

men and with them reinforce Fort Pickens. This seemed
to portend a clash at Pensacola. Many of the *Tribune*'s
readers were alarmed, and so was the General in Chief
of the armies. Excitedly, Scott protested to Lincoln.
Now that the word was out, the order must be can-
celed, Scott said. Otherwise, the Confederates might be
provoked to forestall the government by assaulting
Pickens and also Sumter.

This was not all. Lincoln now learned that Scott had
prepared a memorandum which read: "It is doubtful
. . . whether the voluntary evacuation of Fort Sumter
alone would have a decisive effect upon the States now
wavering between adherence to the Union and secession. It is known, indeed, that it would be charged to
necessity, and the holding of Fort Pickens would be
adduced in support of that view. Our Southern friends,
however, are clear that the evacuation of both forts
would instantly soothe. . . ." Let Sumter go *and Pickens
too!*

The idea gave Lincoln (as he was himself to say) a
"cold shock." Never had the thought occurred to him
that he ought to abandon the Pensacola fort. Never had
it crossed his mind that he ought not to reinforce
Pickens, no matter what he might decide to do about
Sumter. With regard to Pickens the only question was
whether the place actually had been reinforced. He
wondered whether his earlier message had ever reached
the *Brooklyn.* As yet, he had received no reply. If, in
the circumstances, anything needed to be done, it was
to send new orders and even extra reinforcements, not
to cancel the old orders or to abandon the fort. Scott

did not pretend, in the case of Pickens, that reinforcement and retention were impossible for military reasons, as he had argued in the case of Sumter. Scott now was talking like a Virginia politician, not like a military expert. It was enough to make Lincoln doubt that he ever should have listened to his general in chief.

That same day the Senate was scheduled to adjourn. All along, the continuing session had provided a forum for Confederate sympathizers like Senator J. C. Breckinridge of Kentucky (the candidate of the Southern Democrats in the election of 1860). Breckinridge was fond of making speeches in which he called for information about Lincoln's policy, deprecated the idea of "coercion," and blamed the North for obstinately refusing to consider compromise. The Senate's adjournment would not silence men like Breckinridge, but it would take from them their Washington sounding board. It would leave Lincoln with a somewhat freer hand to proceed as he might see fit.

And yet not quite a free hand, at that. Before the session ended, Senator Lyman Trumbull of Illinois introduced the following resolution: "Resolved, that in the opinion of the Senate, the true way to preserve the Union is to enforce the laws of the Union . . . and that it is the duty of the President . . . to use all the means in his power to hold and protect the public property of the United States, and enforce the laws thereof. . . ." Senator Trumbull spoke neither as a fanatic nor as a foe of the President. On the contrary, he was, as politicians went, a reasonable man, and he was a personal friend of Lincoln's—he had been a dependable ally ever since the time of the Lincoln–Douglas contest in 1858. Trumbull now spoke for the majority of Republicans throughout the North. His resolution served as a reminder that, though the Senate no longer watched, Lincoln could disregard the rising Republican sentiment only at the party's peril, and at his own. The resolution served also as at least a partial reply to the latest counsel of General Scott.

That evening Lincoln held his first state dinner. Scott, though present in the White House, did not attend: he was "indisposed." The rest of the company thoroughly enjoyed themselves. There was a babel of small talk around the table, except when their host spoke up, and then they listened attentively to his jokes and stories, and laughed without restraint. Lincoln appeared to be in rare good humor.

But, underneath, he was not in a good humor at all. When the guests were beginning to go, he quietly drew his cabinet members into the Red Room. There he told them, with emotion he obviously was trying to hold back, that General Scott had recommended the evacuation of Pickens as well as Sumter. They were silent, as if stunned. Finally Blair spoke up to denounce Scott for "playing politician." Lincoln, before dismissing the group, asked them to appear for a regular cabinet meeting the next day.

That night he could not get to sleep. Dilemmas do not make for drowsiness, and almost all his information and advice had now piled up on one side or the other of a horrible dilemma. On the one hand, he could not simply let Sumter go. That would settle nothing, for

the Southerners would immediately demand Pickens.
and after that the remaining forts, and there would be
no end to the demanding and the yielding until he had
accepted disunion and recognized the Confederacy—
if, indeed, there would be an end to trouble even then.
On the other hand, if he should try to send supplies to
Sumter, there would be violence, for (as Hurlbut had
emphasized) the Carolinians would certainly resist
even if he should dispatch a ship that was known to
contain "*only provisions.*" There was, perhaps, the glim-
mer of a way between the two alternatives. There was
that suggestion (from James Watson Webb) that Lincoln announce the sending of supplies and then secretly
send troops also, with an empty, decoy vessel to draw
the first fire from the Confederates. But when the other
vessels pushed ahead, the secret would automatically
come to light. *He,* Lincoln, might appear to have been
the aggressor. And in his inaugural he had assured the
Southerners that *they* would have to be the aggressors
if there was to be a war.

The next morning—Good Friday—he got up with a
sense of terrible depression. He was, as he remarked,
"in the dumps."

At noon the cabinet met. There began some talk
about Fort Sumter and also about Fort Pickens and
Scott's amazing advice with regard to it. The conversation seemed to be getting nowhere. So Bates proposed
that Lincoln state his questions and that the members
write down and, one by one, read their answers to the
cabinet. Lincoln then asked for views on Scott's proposal to give up Pickens and on a new proposal for

dealing with Sumter, namely, "to send an armed force off Charleston with supplies of provisions and reinforcements for the garrison at Fort Sumter," and to communicate, "at the proper time, the intentions of the government to provision the fort, peaceably if unmolested." This proposition (a modification of Webb's suggestion) was more complex than the one (merely to send provisions) he had put to his cabinet two weeks earlier and the majority had disapproved.

Bates led off with his opinion, and the others followed. All, without exception, favored holding Fort Pickens. Two, Bates and Smith, were vague on the Sumter question. Not only Blair but also three of his colleagues—Chase, Welles, and Cameron—clearly and strongly seconded Lincoln's Sumter proposal. Seward alone remained in definite opposition. The cabinet vote this time was the reverse of what it had been before. It was a victory for Blair if not also for his get-tough policy: "SC is the head and front of this rebellion," he had just declared, "& when that State is safely delivered from the authority of the US it will strike a blow against our authority from which it will take us years of bloody strife to recover." Seward was in defeat—but (as will be seen) not yet willing to surrender.

None of the cabinet members had indicated that he expected peace to continue. Welles and Chase had made it clear they both thought war likely to result. "But armed resistance to a peaceable attempt to send provisions to one of our own forts," Welles had stated, "will justify the government in using all the power at its command to reinforce the garrison and furnish the necessary supplies." And Chase had said: "If war is to be the result I perceive no reason why it may not be best begun in consequence of military resistance to the efforts of the administration to sustain troops of the Union stationed, under authority of the Government, in a Fort of the Union, in the ordinary course of service." Seward himself did not expect to avoid war by means of the alternative policy he had proposed: he only thought Pickens a better place than Sumter for the fighting to begin, and he "would at once and at any cost prepare for a war at Pensacola and Texas."

After the cabinet meeting, on the same March 29, Lincoln began to act as commander in chief. He drew up orders to Cameron and Welles for army and navy cooperation in preparing a Sumter expedition. Only two weeks or so were left. (This very day, at Sumter, Captain Doubleday was writing to his wife: "If Government delays many days longer it will be very difficult to relieve us in time, for the men's provisions are going fast.") So Lincoln, in his orders, specified that the expedition "be got ready to sail as early as the 6th of April next." Any later than that might be too late.

Lincoln also indicated in some detail the make-up of the expedition. For the Navy Department he ordered: "Stmrs Pocahontas at Norfolk, Pawnee at Washington, and Revenue Cutter Harriet Lane at N. York to be ready for sea with one months stores. Three hundred seamen to be ready for leaving the receiving ship at N. York." And for the War Department: "Three hundred men at N. York ready to leave garrison—one years stores to be put in a portable form."

Then Lincoln hurried Gustavus Vasa Fox off to New York to supervise the preparations there.[2]

3

"I WOULD call Capt. M. C. Meigs forthwith," Seward had said in his March 29 cabinet memorandum. "Aided by his counsel I would at once and at any cost prepare for a war at Pensacola and Texas, to be [under]taken however only as a consequence of maintaining the possession and authority of the United States."

Montgomery C. Meigs was a forty-five-year-old graduate of West Point and a captain in the army corps of engineers. For several years he had been supervising public works in and near Washington, and at the moment he was in charge of the construction at the Capitol. During the past winter he had visited Pensacola and gained a personal knowledge of the fortifications there.

Before the day was over, Seward sent for Meigs and took him to see Lincoln. Meigs began by telling Lincoln that Sumter was "not the place to make the war," but Lincoln did not appear to be interested in Meigs' views on Sumter. Lincoln proceeded to talk about Pickens instead. As long ago as March 5, he now recalled, he had "verbally directed" that this fort be reinforced from the ship already there, the *Brooklyn.* Several days later, finding that nothing had been done, he "had thought it best to put himself on record and had repeated the order in writing." Since then he had "learned that the *Brooklyn* had gone to Key West and as she had the troops for Pickens on board he supposed that his orders had fizzled out." Now Lincoln wanted to know, from Meigs, whether anything could be done to make sure of holding Pickens. He seemed much relieved when Meigs told him that the fort certainly could be held—if it had not been lost already. He requested Meigs to make plans for holding it.

From the White House, Meigs walked home with Seward, who seemed pleased by the outcome of the Lincoln interview. The administration had been "in a strait," Seward explained to Meigs, who recorded the conversation in his diary. "Gen. Scott objected to relieving Fort Sumter or Pickens, thought it best to give them up and thus put a stop to all cry of coercion. For his own [Seward's] part, his policy had been all along to give up Sumter as too near Washington and leaving a temptation to [Jefferson] Davis to relieve it by an [attack] on Washington. That he wished to hold Pickens, making the fight there and in Texas"—where he hoped the Unionist governor, Sam Houston, would co-operate—"and thus make the burden of the war, which all men of sense saw must come, fall upon those who by rebellion provoked it."

Next morning, Saturday, the continuing tension noticeably affected Lincoln. He woke up with a bad sick headache, and after getting out of bed he "keeled over," as Mrs. Lincoln phrased it. His migraine prostrated him all day.

On Easter Sunday he revealed other symptoms of his accumulating anxieties. He was touchy. His temper flared when a group of California politicians called to present a paper criticizing his close friend Senator Baker, of Oregon, and objecting to Baker's influence in the distribution of government jobs. Lincoln tore up the paper, threw the pieces into the fireplace, told his visitors what he thought of them, and showed them unceremoniously to the door. At half past two Captain Meigs and Colonel Keyes (Scott's military secretary) arrived with their draft of a Pickens project, to show it to Lincoln. "He with some effort directed us to read our papers," Meigs noted, "and then ordered us to see Gen. Scott, tell him instructions of the President and that he wished this thing done and not to let it fail. . . ."

On Monday, April 1, Lincoln received confirmation of his fears that the *Brooklyn* had never got his message. A letter, dated March 21, had at last arrived from Captain Israel Vogdes, in command of the troops on board the ship. "Our means of communication with the Government are very uncertain," Vogdes had written. "We do not feel certain that our communications have reached the Department, nor do we know whether the Department's messenger to us may not have been intercepted." Vogdes also indicated his concern about the truce arrangement at Pensacola: it gave "every advantage to the seceders," he said. "They are not required to give any notice of its abrogation, and may attack the fort without a moment's notice." Vogdes' letter made the dispatching of additional aid to Fort Pickens seem all the more urgent.

In a room adjoining Lincoln's office, two men with clerical assistants busied themselves in completing

plans for a Pickens expedition and, finally, drawing up
orders for the President to sign. One of the two men
was Meigs and the other was David D. Porter, a dash-
ing, energetic young naval lieutenant. As the first step
in the proposed plan, Lieutenant Porter was to hasten
to New York, take a warship, "and proceed to sea and
not draw reign [sic] until he was inside the Pensacola
harbor, to watch the place strictly and to prevent any
boat crossing the harbor with troops" to attack Fort
Pickens. As a second step, a troop transport with reinforcements for the fort would follow as soon as possible.
"Should a shot be fired at you," the transport commander was to be instructed, "you will defend yourself
and your expedition at whatever hazard, and if needful
for such defense, inflict upon the assailants all the dam-
age in your power within the range of your guns." Lincoln signed the orders when they were put before him.
Immediately a telegram went off to the New York Navy
Yard: "Fit out *Powhatan* to go to sea at the earliest
possible moment."

It was four weeks, to the day, since Lincoln's inauguration. Now two expeditions were being got ready,
one for Sumter and another for Pickens. In a sense, the
first of these was Blair's, for Blair had sponsored it and
provided its commander, Fox, who now was reporting
back to him. The second was Seward's, for he had
urged it and set its preparation going, and to him its
officers continued to look. Yet both were Lincoln's, for
he was ultimately responsible for both (and indeed he
had had an intimate part in the planning of the Sumter
one). All his advisers could have gone on forever pre-

senting arguments or countering them or balancing them. But it was up to him to act, and action required decision. At last he had decided. At last he was taking action.[3]

4

BLAIR was disgusted. On April 1 he came to the White House with bad news about his Sumter expedition. He had just received two letters that Fox had sent by special messenger from New York. The letters told of frustrations and delays in Fox's efforts to get ships and provisions ready to go to Sumter. He had depended on William H. Aspinwall, a leading New York shipowner, to make available one of his passenger steamers, the *Baltic*, for use as a troop transport. And he had depended on a Captain Marshall to procure provisions. Now both men were holding back.

"From being for a long time most earnest in this matter," Fox wrote to Blair, "they are now astonished at the idea of Govt attempting it, declaring that the time is past and that the people are reconciled to leaving this position and making the stand on Pickens &c." One night Fox argued with the two men till early morning. They finally agreed to co-operate with him on the condition that he postpone his preparations. On Tuesday, April 2, the government was scheduled to float a loan on the money markets of New York. "Mr. A. and Capt.

M. say the loan would not be taken if this news leaked out"—and they feared the news would certainly leak out if active preparations began beforehand.

Later Fox learned that Marshall had reconsidered and, apparently, would have nothing to do with the Sumter project, now or later. "This is serious, as he was expected to obtain all the provisions in what is called the desiccated form," Fox explained to Blair. "These would occupy only half the space of others, could all be carried in bags, in the boats, facilitating the landing and giving the garrison, always, fresh provisions." Fox was sure that Aspinwall's hesitancy about the project and Marshall's opposition to it were "all political" in motivation. "Capt. Marshall has been in Washington for two weeks and wishes to know if Mr. Seward goes for it." Seward's influence again! Fox confessed that he was "heart sick" as the result of "the delays, obstacles and brief time allowed for a vital measure that should have had months' careful preparations."

Lincoln already knew of Aspinwall's stand. The same messenger who had brought Fox's letters to Blair had also brought a letter from Aspinwall to Lincoln. In it Aspinwall told Lincoln he had taken the responsibility of advising Fox, who did not yet have full written instructions from Lincoln, to defer acting until he received them.

"I did so from the conviction," Aspinwall explained, "that were it even suspected that you contemplated reinforcing Fort Sumter . . . the bids for the loan on Tuesday, if they reached the amount offered, would be at rates which Gov. Chase [Secretary of the Treasury

Chase] would hesitate to accept—certainly below 90.

"There are other considerations which prompted me," Aspinwall continued, ". . . a regret that the attempt to reinforce Fort Sumter should now be made, against the odds which have been allowed to accumulate since the early part of February. . . .

"What would be the influence on the money lenders if immediately after a loan was taken, an attempt be made, likely to lead to civil war?

"The public mind is fully prepared for the evacuation of Fort Sumter. . . .

"The relief of Fort Pickens and other feasible efforts to hold what is tenable would in my opinion strengthen the administration & give courage to the Union men of the South."

That argument Lincoln had heard many times from Seward. It did not deter him now. He told Blair to communicate with Fox. Promptly Blair dashed off a note and mailed it, then sent a telegram: "Come on as the President wishes to consult you about the shape of the orders." Blair was reassured.[4]

5

MEANWHILE, by April 1, Seward was growing desperate. True, his Pickens project was going ahead, and if it should succeed he would win back something of his prestige and importance within the administration. But so was the Sumter project going ahead, and this one, unless it were stopped, would discredit and humiliate him. For, all along, he had been promising border-state men, the Confederate commissioners, and others that Sumter would be evacuated. The deadline (March 28), which the commissioners had set for an official audience, went by. Through their go-between, the Supreme Court Justice John A. Campbell, Seward continued to reassure them. On March 30, Campbell left with him a telegram from the governor of South Carolina, Francis W. Pickens, who wanted to know why the Sumter evacuation was being delayed. Lamon, the Governor said, had led him to expect it before now. Seward told Campbell that he, Seward, would have to confer with the President and could not give a definite reply until April 1.

That day Campbell called on Seward again, and Seward informed him that Lincoln was much disturbed by the Governor's telegram with its reference to Lamon's pledge, for Lincoln had given Lamon no authority to commit the government. Campbell asked what he should report to the commissioners. Seward said the President might desire to provision Sumter but would not do so without announcing it beforehand. Campbell insisted upon an authoritative statement, one that really represented the policy of the administration. So Seward went to see the President once more. When he returned he wrote down this sentence for Campbell to take to the commissioners: "I am satisfied the government will not undertake to supply Fort Sumter without giving notice to Governor Pickens." Campbell was satisfied. He did not know that the government already was preparing a Sumter expedition, and Seward did not tell him.

Seward kept worrying. War was on the way. It was bound to result from either the Sumter or the Pickens undertaking, he was sure, but he believed there would be a great difference between the Sumter and the Pickens consequences. He was particularly concerned, as always, about the probable reaction of the non-seceded slave states. He was positive that a Sumter clash would throw most of those states, if not all of them, into seceding and joining the Confederacy. He was sanguine, however, that a Pickens clash would not have nearly so disastrous an effect. The difference was that, somehow, Sumter had come to be looked upon as a party question, even a slavery question. The antislavery Republicans were identified with the policy of coercion at Charleston, the cradle of secession. Pickens did not have such associations. If the issue were drawn at Pensacola (and Texas), and only there, it could be made to seem strictly a matter of patriotism or treason, of *"Union or Disunion."* So Seward reasoned.

There were means by which the war could be limited, shortened, perhaps even averted, he thought. The first step, of course, would be to call off the Sumter project. The next step would be to launch a positive, active foreign policy. This would not be simply a matter of preventing a civil war by starting a foreign war, though there might be merit in that time-tested panacea. Seward had something more specific in mind. Spain, in 1861, had just begun the reconquest of her former West Indian possession, Santo Domingo. A war against

Spain could be expected to appeal to Americans and especially to Southerners. Many Southerners had long wished to get Cuba as additional slave territory. As soon as the United States declared war against Spain, they would want to join in the campaign to overrun Santo Domingo, Puerto Rico, and Cuba. They dare not stay out of such an adventure, for if they did, the North alone would conquer Cuba, and it would become a bastion of free soil. To prevent that from happening, to share in the West Indian conquests, the Confederates might even sacrifice their claims to independence.

These ideas seemed so good to Seward, in his extremity, that he had his son Frederick write out for Lincoln a long memorandum entitled "Some Thoughts for the President's Consideration." The government, Seward brashly began, was utterly "without a policy either domestic or foreign." He proposed a domestic policy: *"Change the question before the Public from one upon Slavery, or about Slavery, for a question upon Union or Disunion."* In other words, abandon Sumter but reinforce and defend Pickens and the other forts on the Gulf of Mexico. Seward also proposed a foreign policy: Demand explanations from Spain, and France as well, at once. Prepare for war with one or both of those countries. He concluded with the gratuitous advice that "whatever policy we adopt, there must be an energetic prosecution of it," and with the generous offer of his own leadership. Somebody, he indicated, must take command.

On one of his visits to the White House, that April Fools' Day, Seward handed his memorandum to Lincoln. And that evening Lincoln wrote out a reply Seward's foreign policy suggestions he ignored. As for a domestic policy, he patiently explained that the administration already had one. It was the very same policy stated in his inaugural: to "hold, occupy, and possess. . . ." He reminded Seward: "This had your distinct approval at the time; and, taken in conjunction with the order I immediately gave General Scott, directing him to employ every means in his power to strengthen and hold the forts, comprises the exact domestic policy you now urge, with the single exception, that it does not propose to abandon Fort Sumpter." Thus Lincoln emphasized that he would not consider a Sumter-for-Pickens deal. Anyhow, "I do not perceive how the re-inforcement of Fort Sumpter would be done on a slavery, or party issue, while that of Fort Pickens would be on a more national, and patriotic one." A final word: true, some definite policy must be executed, the government must be led, but "if this must be done, *I* must do it."[5]

6

SEWARD, though chastened, was not silenced. He still hoped to talk Lincoln into sacrificing Fort Sumter, and he almost succeeded in doing so.

Many Republicans throughout the North apparently agreed with Seward, and several of them, besides the

New York shipowner Aspinwall, sent their opinions to Lincoln. From Maine, for example, the prominent party man Neal Dow wrote that the evacuation of Fort Sumter would be "fully approved by the entire body of Republicans in this State—and I doubt not in all the Country." It would be accepted, Dow said, as "a Military *Necessity*," but he hoped that no such necessity existed in the case of Fort Pickens. From Illinois a Republican wrote: "We (the people of the West) have accepted the evacuation of Fort Sumter as a military necessity. But you & your Cabinet cannot imagine our chagrin at the report of the probable evacuation of Fort Pickens. . . ." From New York a fellow partisan wrote: "If necessity is on you to order the evacuation, history will tardily but firmly and fully justify an act which a villainous administration [Buchanan's] made inevitable."

But other Republican correspondents disagreed. "If you do not mean to recognize the 'Confederacy' the Fort ought to be retained," Lincoln's old friend Owen Lovejoy, brother of the martyred abolitionist Elijah Lovejoy, wrote from Princeton, Illinois. "How long is this to last?" a Philadelphian demanded. "There never has been any other than one proper way of dealing with traitors—destruction to all who oppose the laws!"

If Lincoln could be absolutely sure of holding Pickens, he possibly could afford to reconsider and let Sumter go, but in the circumstances he could not be absolutely sure of holding Pickens. Still, perhaps he could afford to give up Sumter if he could get something else in exchange. Weeks earlier he had remarked that a fort for a state would not be a bad bargain. Fort Sumter for the state of Virginia—was there any real possibility of such a bargain being made?

Seward seemed to think so. He continued to insist that Virginia and indeed all the states of the Upper South were full of Unionists, at least potential ones. If only Lincoln, even now, could talk face to face with the Virginia Unionist leader, Seward's friend George W. Summers . . .

On Tuesday, April 2, Seward sent for a man to be given the delicate mission of going to Richmond and inviting Summers to Washington. The man was Allan B. Magruder, a Washington lawyer, a Virginian, and a Unionist. Seward brought Magruder to the White House and introduced him to Lincoln. Then, with Lincoln's authorization, Magruder left promptly for Richmond.

Early Thursday morning, April 4, Magruder got back to Washington. With him came not Summers, who had been too busy to leave Richmond, but another member of the Virginia convention, John B. Baldwin. Before noon, Magruder and Baldwin called upon Seward at the Department of State. Seward escorted Baldwin to the White House. As soon as Lincoln was free, Seward took Baldwin to the presidential office and, in a confidential whisper, introduced him. Then Seward left.

In search of privacy, Lincoln led Baldwin through several rooms until he found an empty one, a bedroom. He locked the door and drew up two chairs. He began to talk cordially but, from Baldwin's point of view, rather vaguely, even mysteriously. He said something about its being almost too late. Baldwin wondered—too late for what? Lincoln asked why the Unionists did not adjourn the Virginia convention and go home. (They were in the majority, if all the delegates opposed to immediate secession be considered Unionists. This same day the convention was voting two to one against immediate secession.) Baldwin thought there would be no point in the Unionists' bringing about an adjournment, for the secessionists might then call a new, more radical convention. Lincoln indicated that he might have to evacuate Fort Sumter because of military necessity. Baldwin proceeded to lecture him on what the President ought to do: announce an intention to withdraw from both Fort Sumter and Fort Pickens, call a national convention, issue a proclamation promising justice to all, give guarantees that would bring back the seceded states.

Somehow the conversation, which had begun with good will on both sides, became more and more unpleasant, more and more confused. It ended with complete misunderstanding on both sides. Lincoln thought he had made it clear to Baldwin that he was making an offer: a fort for a state. On the one hand, he had hinted that he might find it necessary, for military reasons, to give Sumter up. On the other hand, he had suggested that the Virginians adjourn their convention and thus demonstrate their determination not to secede. This proposition, he concluded, had been rejected out of hand, and further concessions had been required of him. As for Baldwin, he never got the point that Lincoln had intended to make. He went away believing that Lincoln had done no more, and had meant to do no more, than urge the Virginia convention to adjourn. To him this made no sense.

The Baldwin interview was enough to convince Lincoln that his doubts about Virginia Unionism were thoroughly justified. To him the so-called Virginia Unionists were "white crows"—a contradiction in terms. "Yes!" he once exclaimed sarcastically, "your Virginia people are good Unionists, but it is always with an *if!*" If the government would sit still while its property was taken, if the government would give up its forts, let its revenues be cut off, and forget about its laws, then those people might stay in the Union—at least until they changed their minds. Otherwise, they would go for secession and the Confederate States of America! The Union, it seemed, stood to gain little or nothing from Lincoln's bargaining with the Virginians on their terms.

That afternoon, April 4, Lincoln got together with Fox, to make final plans for the Sumter expedition.[6]

7

FOX had become increasingly discouraged after his return to Washington for the shaping of his orders. He had begun to doubt whether his expedition ever would get off. "Delay, indecision, obstacles. War will commence at Pensacola," he confided to a friend. "There the Government is making a stand.

. . ." The government would have to hurry if it was to make a stand at Charleston also. It seemed already too late for the Sumter expedition to sail "as soon as April 6," the time set in Lincoln's original orders of March 29. The delay, the indecision, the obstacles, Fox suspected, were due as usual to Seward's baleful influence.

"As Major Anderson's supplies would be utterly exhausted on the 15th of April," Fox recorded later, "every effort was made by some strong hand to delay the expedition until its supporters must give it up. The last card was to send for a man from the Virginia Convention and say to him that Sumpter would be evacuated at once if the Union people, who were a majority in the Convention, would adjourn it. This Union man declined the proposition and made so many preposterous demands that the President decided the expedition should go forward."

Now, on the afternoon of April 4, Fox and Lincoln put the finishing touches on their Sumter planning. Fox intended the expedition to consist of one passenger steamer (the *Baltic*), three tugboats, two warships (the *Pocahontas* and the *Pawnee*), and the revenue cutter *Harriet Lane*. On the *Baltic* he planned to take ten boats, three hundred sailors to man them, and arms, ammunition, food, coal, and about two hundred soldiers for the fort. In consultation with Secretary of the Navy Welles, Fox impressed upon him the need for powerful naval armament—the need, for example, to have the heaviest howitzers available put on the warships for use in the tugs. "The vital point in my opinion is a naval force that can destroy their [the Confederates'] naval preparations." Welles co-operated fully. He offered to add the formidable war steamer *Powhatan* to the flotilla and suggested that the *Powhatan* carry the three hundred sailors. Fox readily accepted. He and Welles arranged for the various vessels to depart at different times and places and ultimately to rendezvous off Charleston Harbor. From that point Fox intended to try and run in supplies—by the three tugs if the night should be dark and stormy, by the ten boats if it should be clear and still.

But Lincoln did not have in mind such a surreptitious attempt as that. He planned, rather, to be quite open about the undertaking. He was going to notify the governor of South Carolina, in advance, that the expedition was on the way and would provision the fort peaceably, if unmolested.

Of course, Lincoln had little reason to suppose that the Confederates would not be inclined to resist. They would try to stop an approaching Union vessel even if it were known to contain *"only provisions,"* his emissary to Charleston, Hurlbut, had reported to him recently. As long ago as January they had, in fact, fired upon Buchanan's relief ship, the chartered steamer *Star of the West.* Only yesterday, April 3, they had fired upon the schooner *R. H. Shannon,* bound from Boston to Savannah with a cargo of ice. The schooner's captain, who read no newspapers and knew little of current events, had sailed innocently into Charleston Harbor to get away from fog. When he heard the warning shot, he ran up the Stars and Stripes to show that he was all right. Immediately a heavy cannonade opened on him.

Mystified, he took down his flag, and the firing ceased.

Now, if Fox were merely to send in boats or tugs, unannounced, there could be no doubt that the Charleston batteries would open up on them too. But since advance notice was to be given (to the South Carolina governor), there was at least the possibility that, upon careful consideration, the Confederate authorities would decide to withhold their fire. If so, well and good. If not, they would have to shoot first. They, not Lincoln, would have to bear the obloquy of aggression.

To Lincoln it was of the utmost importance that the point be made crystal clear. Therefore he directed that Fox, after his rendezvous off Charleston Harbor, should begin by sending in toward Sumter a boat with provisions but with no armaments. Fox should give the boat's pilot the following orders:

"I send you to Fort Sumpter with a load of provisions to be delivered with a letter to Major A. when you will immediately return. If you are fired upon going in, turn back at once. If any one opposes your entrance deliver to that person the letter addressed to Gov. Pickens and return—if your entrance is still opposed."

The letter to be delivered (if possible) to Major Anderson said only: "Herewith I commence sending you the subsistence entrusted to my charge to be delivered at Fort Sumpter."

The letter addressed to Governor Pickens read: "The U. S. Government has directed me to deliver a quantity of provisions to Major Anderson at Fort Sumpter, due notice of which has probably been given to you by special messenger from Washington. Accordingly I send herewith the first load. *If your batteries open fire it will be upon an unarmed boat, and unarmed men performing an act of duty and humanity.*"

If the batteries should open fire on the unarmed boat, Fox then, according to Lincoln's plan, should call upon all the firepower available to him in order to blast his way into the harbor. Lincoln told Fox (in the final instructions which Lincoln prepared and Cameron signed) that, if his provisioning effort should be opposed, he should report to the senior naval officer on the ships waiting offshore. This officer "will be instructed by the Secretary of the Navy to use his entire force to open a passage, when you will, if possible, effect an entrance and place both troops and supplies in Fort Sumter."

Fox rejoiced. At last his expedition was going ahead! Yet he had misgivings, for there was so much to be done, and so little time in which to do it. He reminded Lincoln that this was April 4 and Anderson's deadline April 15. Fox expected to be able to make his provisioning attempt before that, on April 11 or 12. Even so, he might be too late. He might fail. But Lincoln calmly observed that he would best fulfill his duty by making the attempt anyhow. Fox agreed. With Lincoln's reassurance, he left the White House to make last-minute arrangements in Washington before taking a train to New York the next day.

Not long after bidding Fox farewell, Lincoln was handed a letter that Anderson had mailed from Fort Sumter three days earlier. In it Anderson asked what he should do with the laborers who were still at work constructing the fort—and who still had to be fed. "Having been in daily expectation, since the return of Colonel Lamon to Washington, of receiving orders to vacate this post, I have kept these men here as long as I could," Anderson explained. "I told Mr. Fox that if I placed the command on short allowance I could make the provisions last until after the 10th of this month; but as I have received no instructions from the Department that it was desirable I should do so, it has not been done. If the governor [of South Carolina] permits me to send off the laborers we will have rations enough to last us about one week longer."

From this it appeared that Fox, in assuming April 15 to be the time limit, had been too optimistic. He must have misunderstood Anderson. The limit was not the 15th, not even the 10th, but possibly the 8th—if Anderson had succeeded in getting rid of the workmen. No more than four days left!

At once Lincoln drafted a message to Anderson. This was not to be the evacuation order that Anderson so impatiently awaited. Far from it.

"Your letter of the 1st instant occasions some anxiety to the President," Lincoln began, writing in the third person.

"On the information of Captain Fox he had supposed you could hold out till the 15th instant without any great inconvenience; and he had prepared an expedition to relieve you before that period.

"Hoping still that you will be able to sustain yourself till the 11th or 12th instant, the expedition will go forward; and, finding your flag flying, will attempt to provision you, and, in case the effort is resisted, will endeavor also to re-enforce you.

"You will therefore hold out, if possible, till the arrival of the expedition.

"It is not, however, the intention of the President to subject your command to any danger or hardship beyond what, in your judgment, would be usual in military life; and he has entire confidence that you will act as becomes a patriot and a soldier, under all circumstances.

"Whenever, if at all, in your judgment, to save yourself and command, a capitulation becomes a necessity, you are authorized to make it."

This draft was transmitted to the War Department. There it was copied in quadruplicate. One of the copies, signed by Cameron, was mailed promptly that same day, April 4, to Fort Sumter.[7]

4. Action

1

IT was nearly midnight, April 5, but Lincoln was not yet in bed. He was surprised to have callers at this hour, and still more surprised to learn their errand. Here was Gideon Welles, excited, almost apoplectic, Welles the gray-bearded Secretary of the Navy, who usually held his temper in company (and let it go in private, on the pages of his diary). Here was Commodore S. H. Stringham, to back Welles up. And here were Seward and his son, trying to calm Welles, trying to explain.

Their dispute concerned the *Powhatan*, a rather stumpy, thick-set steamer with an old-fashioned paddle wheel but with powerful engines and also powerful weapons: howitzers, rifled field pieces, ten-inch Dahlgrens, and an eleven-inch pivot gun. Indeed, the *Powhatan* was much the most formidable of the Navy's warships available for immediate duty.

Welles's story was this: During the afternoon he had prepared orders for Captain Samuel Mercer to command the Sumter-bound flotilla, with the *Powhatan* as the flagship. He telegraphed instructions for this vessel to be reserved, at New York, for Mercer's use. That evening, after going home to Willard's Hotel, he congratulated himself that everything was set for the Navy's role in the Charleston venture. Later, after eleven, Seward and Fred Seward appeared at his room. They had a telegram from Captain M. C. Meigs, at New York, saying that movements were retarded and embarrassed by conflicting orders from the Secretary of the Navy. Welles wanted to know what this meant. *What* movements? Seward said he supposed it must refer to the *Powhatan* and Lieutenant D. D. Porter's command. Now Welles was puzzled all the more. Porter's command? Porter had no command! Seward said there must be some misunderstanding. The two agreed that they had better call on the President, and Welles routed Commodore Stringham out of his Willard's bed and brought him along.

Seward was confident that the facts would support him, not Welles. The *Powhatan*, of course, had been assigned to the Pickens expedition four days ago, by the orders which Meigs and Porter had drawn up and which the President had endorsed on April 1. But the facts were embarrassing to Seward. They were humiliating and infuriating to Welles, for up to now they had been hidden from him—naval plans had been made without the knowledge of the Secretary of the Navy! And the facts were awkward, to say the least, for Lincoln.

He looked first at Welles and then at Seward. He read the telegram from Meigs. There must be some mistake, he said. He asked Welles if he was sure the

ACTION

Powhatan had been included in the Sumter expedition.
Welles reminded Lincoln that he had shown him, that
same afternoon, his instructions to Captain Mercer.
Yes, said Lincoln, he remembered seeing the orders
and approving them, but he did not remember that
particular ship. Commodore Stringham said Welles was
right. To clinch the point, Welles now went to the Navy
Department and brought back a copy of the orders.

Convinced, Lincoln turned to Seward and told him
the *Powhatan* must be yielded to Captain Mercer. The
Sumter expedition must not be allowed to fail. Seward
hesitated. Was not the Pickens expedition equally important, he asked, and would it not be spoiled if the
Powhatan were detached? There was time enough for
Pickens, Lincoln answered. It could wait. But there
was no time to be lost with regard to Sumter. He directed Seward to wire New York at once and have the
Powhatan put in Mercer's command. Seward attempted
to stall. It would be hard to get a dispatch through to
the Navy Yard at this time of night, he said. Lincoln
insisted. So Seward left to send the telegram.

Then Lincoln talked apologetically to Welles. He
explained that Seward had his heart set on reinforcing
Fort Pickens and that, on Seward's suggestion, he and
Seward had arranged for supplies and reinforcements
to be sent there as well as to Fort Sumter. But he had
not intended for the Pickens expedition to interfere in
any way with the Sumter one. "He took upon himself
the whole blame," Welles noted, "said it was careless-
ness, heedlessness on his part, he ought to have been
more careful and attentive." As Welles left the White

House that night, he held no grudge against Lincoln, but he was bitter toward Seward, who had gone over Welles's head, tried to run the Navy Department, induced the President to by-pass the Navy Secretary—and never offered an apology or even an explanation.

Welles had yet to hear the end of the story, and so had Lincoln. The *Powhatan* was not to be transferred to Captain Mercer, after all. She was not to go to Charleston. Instead, she was to steam away, hurriedly, at about noon, April 6, under the command of Lieutenant Porter, bound for Pensacola.

What happened was this: Seward sent his telegram, all right, early on the morning of the 6th. He addressed it to Porter, and in it he said: "Give the *Powhatan* up to Captain Mercer." But he did not sign it "LINCOLN." He signed it "SEWARD."

Now, if Porter and Meigs had been inclined to question a telegram from the Secretary of the Navy, they would be still more inclined to question one from the Secretary of State. They already had their orders from Lincoln himself, from the commander in chief of the army and the navy. When Seward's telegram reached them in New York, they were troubled because they feared that Commander A. H. Foote of the Navy Yard might overrule them and detain the *Powhatan*. "Still the President says nothing and I must obey his orders; they are too explicit to be misunderstood," Porter insisted to Foote. "I got them from his own hand. He has not recalled them." And Porter wired back to Seward: "I received my orders from the President and shall proceed and execute them."

ACTION

On the same morning of April 6, Seward gave some interesting information to a Charleston-born newspaperman, James E. Harvey. Promptly Harvey began to send a bewildering succession of telegrams to acquaintances in Charleston. "Order issued for withdrawal of Anderson's command." "Great efforts making to reconsider withdrawal, but will fail." "Final order still reserved. No decision reached." "Positively determined not to withdraw Anderson. Supplies go immediately." Seward knew of these telegrams, and he approved of Harvey's sending them. Afterwards he protected Harvey from a Senate investigation and secured his appointment as minister to Portugal.

Seward was so eager for the Pickens expedition to succeed and for the Sumter expedition to fail that, apparently, he tried to keep the one hidden by drawing attention to the other. All along, he had been concerned with insuring absolute secrecy for the Pickens enterprise. That was why he had intended to withhold its details even from Secretary Welles and the Navy Department. He thought the Navy Department was so full of Confederate sympathizers that, otherwise, his plans immediately would leak out.

That afternoon the transport *Atlantic* (like Fox's *Baltic* a chartered passenger ship), with five hundred troops aboard, and with Captain M. C. Meigs at the helm, followed the *Powhatan* out of New York harbor. Once at sea, Meigs wrote exultingly if cryptically to Seward: "When the arrow has sped from its bow it may glance aside, but who shall reclaim it before its flight is finished?"[1]

2

THE TIME had come, by April 6, for Lincoln to dispatch to the governor of South Carolina, as he had planned to do, the official notice that the Sumter expedition would soon be on its way. The bearer of the notice was to be Robert S. Chew, a State Department clerk. Lincoln instructed Chew to proceed to Charleston and—if, by the time he arrived, the fort had not been attacked and the flag of the United States was still flying over it—to procure an audience with Governor Pickens and read him the following statement:

"I am directed by the President of the United States to notify you to expect an attempt will be made to supply Fort-Sumpter with provisions only; and that, if such attempt be not resisted, no effort to throw in men, arms, or ammunition, will be made, without further notice, or in case of an attack upon the Fort." (Lincoln meant, of course, "*except* in case of an attack.")

After reading this to the governor, Chew was to give him a copy of it but was to hold on to the original. Lincoln wished to keep a record of the message in the exact form in which it had been delivered.

Chew, as things turned out, was not to go to Charleston alone. On April 6 a dispatch-bearer, in the uniform of an army captain, arrived in Washington with messages from Fort Sumter. One of these came from Major Anderson and was dated April 4. "The remarks made to me by Colonel Lamon, taken in connection with the tenor of newspaper articles, have induced me, as stated in previous communications, to believe that orders would soon be issued for my abandoning this work," Anderson had written. "Invested by a force so superior that a collision would, in all probability, terminate in the destruction of our force before relief could reach us, with only a few days' provisions on hand . . . in hourly expectation of receiving definite instructions. . . ." Lincoln decided that the dispatch-bearer, Captain Theodore Talbot, should go back to Charleston with Chew, accompany him on the mission to the Governor, and if possible carry a message out to Anderson at the fort. The message was the same as the one that had been mailed to Anderson two days before: you are to be supplied and, in case of resistance, also reinforced; try to hold out until April 11 or 12. This was the original, in Lincoln's own hand. Chew and Talbot left Washington on the evening of April 6.

Before they had departed from the city, another special courier arrived, a naval lieutenant who had been traveling day and night from Pensacola. At three o'clock in the afternoon, very soon after reaching Washington, he appeared with Secretary Welles at the White House. Welles showed Lincoln the letter which the lieutenant had taken from a belt strapped around his body under his shirt. The letter was addressed to Welles from Captain H. A. Adams, the officer in command of the naval force, including the *Brooklyn*, which had been lying off Pensacola for weeks. Captain Adams was reporting that the order of General Scott to Captain Vogdes, dated March 12, to land the troops from the *Brooklyn* and reinforce Fort Pickens, had finally arrived on March 31—but had not been carried out. The reason: Captain Adams, who had long-standing orders from the Navy Department to observe the truce at Pensacola, did not feel like violating those orders on "such insufficient authority as General Scott's order." The navy was not taking directions from the army! But if Secretary Welles should indorse Scott's order, Captain Adams would, of course, act upon it.

Lincoln agreed with Welles that a special messenger must immediately be sent overland with instructions for Captain Adams to co-operate with Captain Vogdes in the landing of the troops. Welles hoped the messenger could take the southbound mail train that evening. But he had to find an absolutely trustworthy man, and it was late that night before he could present the mission to the man he wanted, Lieutenant John L. Worden. Welles then read to Worden the message for Captain Adams, gave Worden a copy of it, and told him to commit it to memory, so that if necessary he could destroy the paper. Early the following morning Worden set out for Pensacola by way of Richmond.[2]

3

TORRENTIAL rain turned the streets of Washington into rivers on Sunday night, April 7. In places the water was a foot deep. Within the shelter of the White House Lincoln sat talking with a visitor from Virginia, the rotund John Minor Botts, who once had been a Whig colleague of Lincoln's in Congress.

Botts had come, with the strong endorsement of Secretaries Bates and Seward, to urge a scheme for preserving, at the last minute, both the Union and the peace. It was a peculiar scheme. Call a convention of all the states, Botts pleaded. Let the convention draw up a constitutional amendment giving the seceded states permission to withdraw from the Union. Allow them to keep the forts and other property but require them to pay a fair price, and if they do not have enough cash, trust them. Within twelve months the people of those states will come to their senses and apply for readmission. Then readmit them, but only on condition that they repudiate the absurdity of secession and promise to behave themselves better in the future. "This will save the *constitutional question*," Botts argued, "and avert the necessity for civil war." Also, according to Botts, it would prevent Virginia and the other states of the Upper South and the border from seceding.

Lincoln listened patiently. When Botts had concluded, Lincoln indicated his doubts. *Would* Virginia remain in the Union if the forts should be given up? Lincoln told Botts of his conversation with Botts's fellow Virginian, John B. Baldwin, three days earlier. He mentioned making a proposition to Baldwin about evacuating Fort Sumter if the Virginia convention would agree to adjourn.

"Well, Mr. Lincoln," Botts asked eagerly, "what reply did Mr. Baldwin make?"

"Oh!" said Lincoln, throwing up his hands, "he wouldn't listen to it at all; scarcely treated me with civility. . . ."

"Mr. Lincoln," Botts broke in, "will you authorize me to make that proposition? for I will start tomorrow morning, and have a meeting of the Union men tomorrow night, who, I have no doubt, will gladly accept it."

Lincoln replied: "It is too late now." He knew that, if all went well, the Sumter expedition would be getting under way by tomorrow night.

There was a pause. Then Lincoln said: "Botts, I have always been an old-line Henry Clay Whig, and if your Southern people will let me alone, I will administer this government as nearly on the principles that he would have administered it as it is possible for one man to follow in the path of another." Another pause. "We have seventy-odd men in Fort Sumter, who are short of provisions. I can not and will not let them suffer for food." Both men were silent, while the rain beat down outside.

"What do I want with war?" Lincoln finally burst out. "I am no war man; I want peace more than any man in this country. . . ."[3]

4

THE next day the rain was still coming down endlessly, and muddy streams continued to whirl along the channels they had made in the Washington streets. The air was clammy and, for April 8, quite warm.

Five weeks had passed since Lincoln's inauguration. Things were beginning to happen: Fox would be setting out from New York tonight or tomorrow. In the mild, moist atmosphere of the capital there was a heightening sense of apprehension and excitement.

John Minor Botts, Lincoln's visitor of last evening, was full of excitement when he reappeared at the White House. He had hurried over to warn Lincoln that Virginia secessionist fanatics were maturing a plot to take the city. Botts, just now, had heard the story from a man who, in turn, had got it direct from one of the plotters.

Lincoln listened attentively. He was not inclined to dismiss the Botts story as a wild rumor. It only seemed to confirm the reports he had been receiving for the past few days. General Scott already possessed evidence that there were "machinations" against the Federal government not only in the distant South but also in nearby Maryland and Virginia. Lincoln requested Botts to ride at once to the General's residence.

Scott had been considering the desirability of Lincoln's calling upon the Northern states for militia to defend the capital. Today he proposed to War Secretary Cameron the requisitioning of ten companies. For the past week he had been submitting, at Lincoln's request, regular daily reports to the President. Now, in his "daily report No. 7," he said: "For the defence of the government more troops are wanted." (He also said that Major Anderson, in a letter received this morning, and dated April 5, showed some "nervous irritability"—the poor Major still was "confidently hoping" that he would "receive ample instructions in time." Scott said, further, that there was "nothing official" from the expeditions out of New York.)

Lincoln, too, had been considering the need for troops. More than that: he had been taking steps to obtain them. He had summoned the governor of Pennsylvania, Andrew G. Curtin, for a confidential talk in Washington, and Curtin had returned to Harrisburg to see if he could get from his legislature a new militia bill and the necessary funds. Now, on April 8, Lincoln prodded Curtin with a telegram: "I think the necessity of being *ready* increases. Look to it."

On this day Seward finally ended his dalliance with the Confederate commissioners. Only yesterday, in another note their go-between delivered, the commissioners had asked for reassurances, first, that no supplies would be sent to Fort Sumter without advance notice and, second, that no change prejudicial to the Confederacy was contemplated with regard to Fort Pickens. Seward had replied: "Faith as to Sumter fully kept; wait and see. . . ." Today, however, he broke off the tenuous relationship he had maintained with the commissioners. He passed on to them his formal answer to their official note of March 12, in which, as the presumed ambassadors from a sovereign government, they had requested a hearing and the beginning of negotiations. His answer flatly denied their presumptions and their requests.

That evening Seward entertained the London *Times* correspondent William H. Russell at home. Seward, his wife, his son, and their guest played whist for a while, but Seward did poorly: his mind was not on the game. He kept talking to his partner, Russell. The government, he said, was going to protect its forts in the South. "But we are determined in doing so to make no aggression. The President's inaugural clearly shadows out our policy. We will not go beyond it—we have no intention of doing so—nor will we withdraw from it."

Seward put down his cards and told his son to bring a portfolio from the study. Mrs. Seward let down a droplight, for reading, and lit the gas, then left the room. Seward offered Russell a cigar and began to smoke one himself. He took from the portfolio a dispatch for the British government and proceeded to read it slowly. Russell thought its tone hostile. It seemed to imply that foreign governments had no business to take the slightest notice of secession. "Even war with us," Russell thought, "may not be out of the list of those means which would be available for refusing the broken Union into a mass once more."

Seward resumed his friendly conversation with the Englishman. He minimized the American crisis. It would be all over within three months, he said. There will come a "re-action" before then. "When the Southern States see that we mean them no wrong—that we intend no violence to persons, rights, or things—that the Federal Government seeks only to impose obligations imposed on it in respect to the national property, they will see their mistake, and one after another they will come back into the Union." At midnight Seward was still talking.

Meanwhile, in New York Harbor, just inside of Sandy Hook, Gustavus Vasa Fox, on board the *Baltic*, was waiting for the morning tide. Fox had whiled away the evening by writing letters to his wife and his brother-in-law, Montgomery Blair. "We have just anchored for the night and shall go over the bar at daylight tomorrow evening," he wrote. "We ought to be off Charleston the night of the 11th and make an attempt the night of the 12th." He was determined, though somewhat doubtful. "I cannot shrink from a solemn duty, which, if successful, is pregnant with great results for our beloved country. I am afraid we are too late, from no fault of mine."

They were too few as well as too late, but Fox was not aware of that. He did not know that the *Powhatan*, which was to have carried the three hundred sailors to man his boats, had headed for Pensacola, not Charleston.[4]

5

MORE than three days of waiting followed, for Lincoln, for his colleagues, and for the people of the Union. The people, or at least those who read the newspapers, took it for granted that great events were about to occur. The papers reported the bustle of naval activity in New York Harbor and interpreted it to mean that the administration was making some decisive move. Obviously troops and ships were setting out. Where to? What for? Speculation ranged from South Carolina to Florida to Texas but focused mainly on the first of the three. A rumor ran that, at Fort Sumter, firing already had begun.

It remained to be seen what the papers would say and the people would think once the firing had begun in fact—if it ever should begin at all. Were the people ready to support a policy of force? This question, naturally, was of the utmost concern to Lincoln.

He could count upon the enthusiastic backing of most (though not all) Republicans. This he knew from previous conferences with party leaders and from the letters, still coming in, of party members.

He now heard from Carl Schurz, the German-American leader, whom he recently had seen in Washington and had given permission to prepare confidential reports on public opinion. Writing his first report (April 5), from Milwaukee, Schurz began by referring to the late-March and early-April elections which, in various localities of New England and the Middle West, had gone against the Republicans. These results, Schurz believed, indicated dissatisfaction with the government's seeming uncertainty and inactivity. "On my way home," he wrote, "I have seen New York merchants, New England manufacturers and traders, and farmers of the West, and from personal observation I may say that there is a general discontent pervading all classes of society. Everybody asks: What is the policy of the Administration? And everybody replies: Any distinct line of policy, be it war or a recognition of the Southern Confederacy, would be better than this uncertain state of things." Action, Schurz thought, would change the public mood. "As soon as one vigorous blow is struck, as soon as, for instance, Fort Sumter is reinforced, public opinion in the free States will at once rally to your support."

In his daily mail Lincoln received, from volunteer advisers throughout the North, abundant confirmation of Schurz's main point. "Reinforce Fort Sumter at all hazards and at any cost! . . . one bold stroke . . . strike terror to the hearts of the Rebels in the South!" "If . . . the present administration, by a timely move of shrewdness, or 'audacity' could re-inforce, what an immense moral power would be gained to the nation and the administration. Form, from chaos—light, from darkness." "Give up Sumpter, Sir, & you are as dead politically as John Brown is physically. You have got to fight." "For humanity's sake continue firm energetick and decided. Had you taken the same course 10 days sooner all the Western elections would have been largely Republican." "Give those South Carolina ruffians h——l, and we will support you." But these communications were as partisan as they were patriotic. They came from Republicans.

Such views were not widely shared by Democrats, even in the North. Though, of course, Lincoln had less direct access to Democratic opinion, some of its manifestations were plain enough. Many of the opposition party were outspoken. After listening, as a banker's dinner guest in New York, to the conversation of three of them—the prominent lawyer Samuel J. Tilden, the former (and future) governor Horatio Seymour, and the historian-publicist George Bancroft—the ubiquitous English newsman Russell concluded that "the Government could not employ force to prevent secession." These men "could not bring themselves to allow their old opponents, the Republicans now in power, to dispose of the armed forces of the Union against their brother Democrats in the Southern States."

The Democratic mayor of New York, Fernando Wood, was openly in favor of the city's seceding from the Union and from the state and setting itself up as a free city. The New York Herald was giving editorial approval to Wood's scheme. A secret league of four or five thousand men was said to be conspiring to carry it out. In the circumstances, the risk of war with the South appeared, to some Republicans, to be doubly dangerous. Secretary Chase, in Washington, had a letter from John Jay, in New York, who warned: "The moment hostilities shall break out at the front, we will be in danger of *insurrection at New York.*"

Besides the Democrats in the North, there were Democrats and others in the non-seceded South to be considered. Lincoln had been told, often enough, that "coercion" would cause even the old Whigs of Virginia and the rest of the wavering states to go for secession. But he was advised by Schurz: "Never fear the border States. They speculate upon the weakness of the Government. Every display of strength will disconcert and overawe them."

In view of the widespread anti-coercionist feelings, a clash at Sumter might unite the South and divide the North—unless the occasion for the clash was properly understood. Lincoln needed to see that his policy, at last taking form in action, was presented most carefully to the public. Now that the Sumter expedition was actually setting out, he ordered that news reporters be barred from all departments of the government. He did not, however, prevent the leaking of news about the hoped-for peaceable provisioning of Fort Sumter, or the release of a "semi-official announcement" which one newsman wired to a press association on April 9. This announcement read in part: "Extensive as the military and naval preparations are, it is persistently stated in Administration quarters that they are for defensive purposes only, and that nothing is intended not strictly justified by the laws, which it is the duty of the President to enforce to the extent of his ability. If resistance be made to his efforts in this particular, and bloodshed be the result, the responsibility must fall on those who provoke hostilities; and the assurance of the Inaugural is repeated, that the Administration will not be the aggressor."

Next morning the *New York Tribune* and the *New York Times* announced "positively, and as if by authority" (as one reader of both papers put it), that a fleet was on the way to Charleston. "If the rebels fire at an unarmed supply ship, and make a perfectly proper act the pretext for shedding the blood of loyal citizens, on their heads be the responsibility," the *New York Post* editorialized that evening. "At Charleston, tomorrow, the rebels will elect between peace and war. If they declare for war and shed the blood of loyal men, it only remains for the President to take measures to put down rebellion." Other newspapers throughout the North took the same cue, and so did at least one border-state paper. "The secession leaders are relying very heavily upon the first shock of battle for the promotion of a general secession feeling in the Southern States," the *Louisville Journal* remarked. "If the General Government commit any wrong or outrage upon South Carolina or Florida, it will be condemned; but if a United States vessel shall be fired into and her men slain for a mere attempt to take food to the Government's troops in the Government's own forts, and if war shall grow out of the collision, no spirit of secession or rebellion will be created thereby this side of the cotton line."

Speculation and rumor continued, but they now concerned the policy of Jefferson Davis rather than that of Lincoln. One rumor, on April 11, said that Davis had ordered the Charleston authorities to hold back and permit the provisioning of Sumter. "A politic move," it seemed to a New Yorker, on April 11, "for everything depends on being strictly right on the particular issue in which the first blood is drawn, and many Democrats and Border State men would say the South was wrong in refusing to allow the *status quo* to be maintained by a supply of food to Anderson and his little force."[5]

6

FRIDAY, April 12, 1861. This would surely be the day. Lincoln's policy and his responsibility would be put to the test at any hour now—if indeed the hour had not already come. "God bless you," one sympathizing citizen had written to him. "I am glad I am not President."

Rain continued, off and on, in Washington. This was the backlash of a storm over the Atlantic, a storm which had been raging for two or three days and which, as Scott had reported to Lincoln, "must have been of great violence." Through that storm, Fox and all the vessels of his expedition would have had to make their way.

There had been no late news from Charleston when the cabinet met for a regular midday session. The President appeared to be calm, even rather light-hearted. He told his counselors that he had conferred with the mayor of Washington about construction plans for the west wing of the Treasury Building. He now recommended that the work go ahead—so as to keep the people of the city in a good humor. It was agreed.

The Secretary of War produced a letter from Sam Houston, the governor of Texas. Houston was declining the offer, made to him by the commanding officer of the United States Army in Texas, for troops to be used in saving the state from the secessionists.

The two recent messengers to Charleston, Captain Talbot and R. S. Chew, presented their reports.

First, Talbot recounted their journey. They had arrived in Charleston on the evening of April 8. Talbot called, alone, upon Governor Pickens, and the Governor agreed to receive the President's emissary, Chew. Both Talbot and Chew then visited the Governor, and Chew read him, and gave him a copy of, the President's message—that an attempt would be made to supply Fort Sumter with "provisions only" and that, if this were not resisted, no effort would be made to throw in men, arms, or ammunition. The Governor said he wished to have General P. G. T. Beauregard, of the Confederate States Army, present at the interview, for Beauregard was now in charge of military affairs in the Charleston area. Chew assented. General Beauregard having been called into the room, the Governor read him the message and handed him the copy. Talbot asked the Governor if he could proceed to the fort and remain on duty there. The Governor referred him to the General, and Beauregard peremptorily refused permission. Talbot than asked if he could communicate with Major Anderson. Again Beauregard said No. Talbot and Chew left Charleston at eleven o'clock the same night, but they were delayed by poor rail connections at Florence, South Carolina, and at Richmond, and so they had reached Washington only this morning, the 12th. (They had got through just in time; later in the day, floods were to cut off rail service between Richmond and Washington.)

Talbot brought back with him, still sealed up in its pouch, the letter to Anderson that Lincoln had intrusted to him—the letter informing Anderson that an expedition was on the way to Sumter. Lincoln took this letter and kept it. On the envelope he wrote: "This was sent by Capt. Talbot, on April 6, 1861, to be delivered to Maj. Anderson, if permitted. On reaching Charleston, he was refused permission to deliver it to Major Anderson." Lincoln could have added—but he did not—that the same message had been sent to Anderson two days earlier (April 4), by regular mail.

After Talbot had completed his report to the cabinet, Chew gave his own account, which corroborated Talbot's. Chew added: "In reply to a remark made by Governor Pickens in reference to an answer, I informed him that I was not authorized to receive any communication from him in reply."

The answer would have to come in some other form. Fox, with his flotilla, ought to be off Charleston soon, if not already. The President and the cabinet were waiting. They could expect one or the other of the possibilities that Attorney General Bates envisioned. "If Maj. Anderson hold out . . ." it seemed to Bates, "one of two things will happen—either the fort will be well provisioned, the Southrons forbearing to assail the boats, or a fierce contest will ensue, the result of which cannot be foreseen."[6]

5. Reaction

1

ROME was built on seven hills and so was Montgomery, as its people liked to point out. They saw more than mere coincidence in the fact. If not yet a seat of empire, Montgomery already was the capital of Alabama and of all the cotton states. It was the home of an ambitious, if provisional, essay at government.

Montgomery's Main Street, wide and sandy, sloped up to the capitol hill from the low banks of the Alabama River. Once a rather lazy and sleepy expanse, Main Street now was a bustling thoroughfare. By the fountain in front of the leading hotel an auctioneer offered slaves for sale, as usual, and up and down the street various hucksters peddled other goods. Crowding the street nowadays, however, were newcomers of various kinds—politicians, government workers, jobseekers, contract agents, and miscellaneous adventurers. Talking politics and business, these people argued about what the new government should do and speculated about what it *would* do. They watched for the latest "bulletins" posted outside the Exchange

Hotel, the newspaper office, and the Government House. The suspense began to heighten rapidly during the first week in April.

On the hill, near the neoclassic capitol, stood the President's mansion, a pleasing but unpretentious dwelling with a mock-orange hedge in front of it. Night after night the glow of a lamp could be seen in a window above the hedge, the study window of the busy President. Only a short walk away was a huge red-brick building, formerly a warehouse, which now contained the Confederate offices; this was the Government House. Inside, on the first floor, a large whitewashed hall gave access to a number of small rooms, each of them the headquarters of some bureau. A stairway led to the second floor, where there were other offices. Over one of the doors upstairs a crudely lettered sign read simply: "The President."

When the President rose to greet a visitor—and he had many visitors these days—he stood erect and straight, like the trained soldier that he was, but with more a gentlemanly than a military bearing. He was somewhat taller and much thinner than the average. Unlike most of those around him, he did not chew and spit tobacco, and he looked clean and neat, with trimmed hair and brushed boots. He would have been strikingly handsome had his cheeks not been so hollow, his lips so thin and tightly pressed, and his bad eye so disconcerting. This eye, nearly blind, was partly covered by a filmy growth. Sitting at his desk, in conversation, he had the habit of listening with his eyelids closed, then suddenly opening them and shooting forth a gleam from his good eye. He gave the impression of great self-confidence, despite the lines of tiredness and pain (he suffered from severe neuralgia) in his face.

In his makeshift executive office, Jefferson Davis spent as much as fifteen or sixteen hours a day and then often took work home with him, to read and ponder till early morning, by the lamp that glowed in the window above the mock-orange hedge. Adjacent to his office was the cabinet room, and close by were the rooms of his cabinet advisers. He kept in constant touch with these men.

Each of the seven states had at least one representative in the administration, and Georgia had two—the shriveled, wizened little vice president, Alexander H. Stephens, and his good friend, the big, bluff, jovial secretary of state, Robert Toombs. Alabama was represented by the cautious but dutiful secretary of war, Leroy P. Walker; South Carolina by the German-born poor boy who had risen as a Charleston banker, Secretary of the Treasury Christopher G. Memminger; Louisiana by the colorful, exotic attorney general, Judah P. Benjamin; Florida by the nautically experienced secretary of the navy, Stephen R. Mallory; and Texas by the one-time plantation overseer, Postmaster General John H. Reagan. Mississippi was represented by the President himself.

Davis listened to all his advisers, and especially to Benjamin, but yielded his authority to none of them. He was his own boss. He took particular interest in military affairs, even in the smallest details. Indeed, he ran the War Department himself and left Walker, the nominal secretary of war, with little to do except to transmit presidential orders. This was natural, in view of Davis' previous experience as West Point cadet, professional soldier on the Indian frontier, veteran of the Mexican War, and head of the War Department under President Franklin Pierce. He had behind him a brilliant record both as field tactician and as army administrator.

On the question that increasingly haunted them—would there be peace, or war?—Davis and his advisers thought essentially alike, though differing a bit in their estimates of the probable and the desirable. Benjamin was the frankest in predicting and even welcoming a conflict. "I am still very confident we shall have a collision," he wrote on April 3. Whatever their differences, all agreed upon the following propositions:

(1) Secession was perfectly justified on moral, legal, and constitutional grounds, as well as the grounds of self-interest, and was in itself an entirely peaceable act. (2) The seceded states and the Confederate government, in their behalf, were entitled to take over all the public property and places within their boundaries, the only condition being that the new government reimburse the old for a fair share of construction and improvement costs. (3) The United States government long since had committed the first act of aggression (by authorizing Major Anderson's move from Fort Moultrie to Fort Sumter) and was continuing to commit aggression by its very refusal to yield Sumter and the other forts. (4) Hence the responsibility for

war, if actual war should come, must rest with the Federal government: the decision was up to Lincoln, not Davis.

"When Lincoln comes in," Davis had written privately before resigning from the United States Senate, "he will have but to continue in the path of his predecessor to inaugurate a civil war." Prepare yourselves for a long and bloody conflict unless the Federal government proves willing to grant us peace, he had told the people at station stops on the way to Montgomery for his inauguration. "Anxious to cultivate peace and harmony with all nations, if we may not hope to avoid war, we may at least expect that posterity will acquit us of having needlessly engaged in it," he had said in his inaugural address. "Doubly justified by the absence of wrong on our part, and by wanton aggression on the part of others. . . ."

Yet, for all his phrases, Davis could hardly hide, even from himself, the fact that he doubtless would have a big decision to make. After Lincoln had acted, or perhaps even before, he would have to act. Upon him, too, would depend the issue of peace or war. Like Lincoln, he must decide as best he could in the light of his own preconceptions and in response to public demands.[1]

2

THE CONFEDERACY, in the eyes of its leaders and supporters, was not so much a nation in being as a nation in the process of becoming. Among these people, no one was satisfied with the boundaries as drawn before April 12, 1861. No one had a vision so narrow that he looked only to the seven states whose representatives were meeting in Montgomery. Rather, these would-be nation-builders entertained grand, imperial designs. "We are now the nucleus of a growing power," Vice President Stephens proclaimed (March 21), "which, if we are true to ourselves, our destiny, and high mission, will become the controlling power on this continent."

At the very least, as the most modest of the Southern imperialists envisaged it, the full-grown Confederacy would have to include Virginia, Maryland, and other slaveholding states of the Upper South and the border. Through the accession of Virginia and Maryland the Confederacy would acquire also the District of Columbia and a good claim to a share of all Federal property and Federal territories. Once all the slave states were joined together, as the *New Orleans Picayune* had predicted on the day South Carolina seceded, the "line forming their northern border" would extend westward above all the territory "adapted to the extension of slavery." A large part of the West would thus be "at the control of the united South." "More than this, we absolutely carry with us . . . the District of Columbia, with all the millions of national property within its limits." In addition, the Confederacy of the future "holds the mouth of the Mississippi and has the keys to the commerce of the entire Mississippi and Ohio valley."

The new empire, as expansionists dreamed of it, would stretch not only northward, from the Gulf of Mexico to the Ohio River and the Mason-Dixon Line, but also westward from the Atlantic to the Pacific Ocean. It would embrace the territories of Colorado, New Mexico, Utah, and Arizona, and even the state of California, which presumably could be induced to secede from the Union. Sooner or later the Confederacy might win still other lands from Mexico, Central America, and the Caribbean islands. It might even admit states from the Northwest and, possibly, Pennsylvania and New York besides, though never New England. In comparison, the once proud United States eventually would amount to little.

These were intoxicating thoughts, but April had come, and not one of them had been realized. Not one of them appeared to be on the way to early realization. Virginia still remained aloof from the Confederacy. On April 4 the Virginia convention, which had been elected to consider secession, voted 89 to 45 against it. Until Virginia should leave the Union, none of the other hoped-for states would be likely to do so. Thus, in early April, it appeared that (unless something drastic were done) the Confederacy was doomed to carry on, if possible, as a mere string of seven states, an aborted empire.

What was worse, it appeared that, given time, one or more of the seven might abandon the Confederacy and return to the Union. If, in the lower South, true Unionists or "reconstructionists" were few, they were nevertheless too numerous to suit the thoroughgoing, fire-eating secessionists. Especially in Alabama, the home state of the Confederate government, reconstructionism in one guise or another seemed a threat to Southern independence. The outstanding secessionist William L. Yancey, a resident of Montgomery, had failed to win election to the Confederate Congress. In one Alabama town this "fire-eater" had, in a sense, actually eaten fire: he had been burned in effigy. "We are in danger," the *Charleston Mercury* warned (March 25), "of being dragged back eventually to the old political affiliation with the states and people from whom we have just cut loose."

The Confederate founding fathers strove to present to the outside world an impression of complete unity and harmony—in contrast to the obvious partisan and factional divisions of the North. Underneath the surface, however, the tensions of personal rivalry and political difference were straining the new nation and threatening to tear it apart. In Montgomery itself "every knot of men had its grievances." Critics complained of the government's slowness to organize and get going, the incompetence in the cabinet and the Congress, the favoritism in army appointments, and dozens of other governmental faults, real or imaginary.

Throughout the South old Whigs disliked old Democrats, original secessionists distrusted recent converts, proponents of reopening the African slave trade condemned their opponents, and advocates of an exclusive, slave-based Confederacy denounced those who would open the way to the easy admission of additional states, even free ones.

Political discontent was aggravated by economic uncertainty. Bankers were suspending specie payments, planters and traders bearing an increased burden of debt, manufacturers facing a business slow-down. There was a "feeling that the existing suspense and apprehension were intolerable, and that almost any change would be an improvement." Time, which for weeks had appeared to be on the side of the Confederacy, no longer so appeared. The new nation's prospects deteriorated with delay.

"The country is sinking into a fatal apathy," the *Mobile Mercury* complained, referring to the Southern country, "and the spirit and even the patriotism of the people is oozing out under this do-nothing policy. If something is not done pretty soon, decisive, either evacuation or expulsion, the whole country will become so disgusted with the sham of southern independence that the first chance the people get at a popular election they will turn the whole movement topsy-turvy so bad that it never on earth can be righted again."

Something must be done, and soon. Evacuation or expulsion! Get the Yankees out of the Southern forts! Expulsion might lead to war, of course, but war was by no means the worst of possible evils.

A clash at Sumter would bring Virginia over to the Confederacy at once; this was an axiom of Southern thinking. With Virginia would come Maryland and other slave states, even Delaware. There would then be, most likely, fifteen states in the Confederacy as compared with eighteen in the Union.

War would not only enlarge but it would also inspirit and solidify the Confederacy. So a number of Southerners believed. "There is another way of avoiding the calamity of reconstruction and that is war," an Alabaman said. "Now pardon me for suggesting that South Carolina has the power of putting us beyond the reach of reconstruction by taking Fort Sumter at any cost." Lincoln's investigator Stephen A. Hurlbut noticed similar sentiments at the time of his visit to South Carolina. He wrote: "The power in that State and in the Southern Confederacy is now in the hands of the Conservatives—of men who desire no war, seek no armed collision, but hope and expect peaceable separation, & believe that after separation the two sections will be more friendly than ever." Yet, it seemed to Hurlbut, "it is equally true that there exists a large minority indefatigably active and reckless who desire to precipitate collision, inaugurate war & unite the Southern Confederacy by that means. These men dread the effects of time & trial upon their Institutions."

Interpreting Southern opinion from a Northern point of view, the *Indianapolis Journal* predicted, in April, that hostilities were about to begin. Not because the Lincoln administration desired anything but peace, this newspaper explained. "But because the seceded

States are determined to have war; because they believe a war will drive to support the border slave
States, and unite them all in a great Southern Confederacy. A policy of peace is to them a policy of destruction. It encourages the growth of a reactionary
feeling. It takes out of the way all the pride and re-
sentment which could keep the people from feeling
the weight of taxation, and the distress of their isolated
condition. It forces them to reason, and to look at the
consequence of their conduct. A war buries all these
considerations in the fury and glory of battle, and the
parade and pomp of arms. War will come because the
Montgomery government deems it the best way of
bringing in the border States, and of keeping down
trouble at home."

Certainly, in the belief of the more extreme Southern
patriots, war would serve the Confederacy well. The
war need not be long and bloody. The Confederacy
would go into it with potential strength, the Union
with potential weakness. The one side would have
many friends, the other side many enemies. Great
Britain and France, both of them dependent on Southern cotton, would, if necessary, intervene to get it. The
British would forbid any invasion of Southern soil,
and they would sweep aside any attempted blockade
of Southern ports. Various groups that the United
States had antagonized at one time or another—the
Mexicans, the Mormons, the Indians—would be likely
to help in winning an empire in the West.

These would not be the only friends of the Montgomery government, or foes of the Washington govern-

ment, whom war would arouse. "If, through the madness of Northern Abolitionists, that dire calamity must come," Davis had been told by his New Hampshire friend Franklin Pierce, the former president of the United States, "the fighting will not be along Mason's and Dixon's line merely." The fighting would also be along a line between the "Abolitionists" and their opponents everywhere, even in the Northern streets. "Those who defy law and scout constitutional obligations will, if we ever reach the arbitrament of arms, find occupation enough at home," Pierce was sure. He implied that the sound, conservative Democrats of the North would stand together with the Democrats of the South.

Indeed, the Confederates felt that they had no quarrel with the Northern people as a whole. The enemy would consist only of the "Abolitionists," the "Black Republicans," the "Lincolnites." Those people were cowards. They were mere "mudsills." They had been degraded by their pursuit of gain, by their devotion to commerce, manufactures, and the base mechanical arts. They would never fight unless the odds were overwhelmingly in their favor.

From this whole course of reasoning it followed, in the minds of some Confederates, that if they attacked and took Fort Sumter, this would not provoke a war, after all. Just the opposite: it would provide a guarantee of peace. The divided North would not risk hostilities against a united South. An assault upon Sumter, by bringing over Virginia and the border states, would give the Black Republicans pause. The secession of

Virginia would go far to "prevent Lincoln, Scott and Co. from using force," according to the Georgia leader Howell Cobb. The taking of Sumter would absolutely forestall military action on the part of the North, according to the South Carolina fire-eater Robert Barnwell Rhett.

Understandably, the Carolinians itched to take the fort that flaunted what was to them a foreign flag in their own harbor. They were deterred by no compunctions about aggression, for they were convinced they would be doing no more than returning blow for blow. "Upon the whole it is fortunate," as one Carolinian wrote with reference to Major Anderson's spiking his guns at Moultrie and moving his garrison to Sumter, "that the first act of aggression is removed from the shoulder of our gallant little state." The other seceding states, except Florida, had managed to seize all the Federal property on their soil. Why should South Carolina, the secession pioneer, go on refraining with regard to Sumter? "Let the strife begin," the *Charleston Courier* demanded on April 10, "—we have no fear of the issue."

On that very day two Virginians in Charleston were doing their best to stir up trouble. One was the young and black-haired Roger Pryor, and the other the old and white-haired Edmund Ruffin. Both were fanatical secessionists who feared that their own state would not move until the Charleston guns opened fire. That night the rabble-rousing Pryor addressed a crowd from the balcony of the Charleston Hotel. "I assure you that just as certain as tomorrow's sun will rise upon us," he

declaimed, "just so sure will old Virginia be a member
of the Southern Confederacy; and I will tell your
Governor what will put her in the Southern Confederacy in less than an hour by Shrewsbury clock.
Strike a blow!"[2]

3

BY the beginning of April, the
Davis government already possessed a set policy, of
more than six weeks' standing, for dealing with the
problem of the forts. This policy the Confederate Congress had embodied in secret resolutions (February 15)
that "immediate steps should be taken to obtain possession of Forts Sumter and Pickens . . . either by
negotiation or force." In the spirit of these resolutions,
Davis was using negotiation, or attempts at negotiation, for the twofold purpose of winning the forts
without war, if possible, and of gaining time for military preparations in case a resort to force should become necessary. Meanwhile he was doing his best to
speed the preparations of the Confederacy and to
co-ordinate and control those of the separate states.

The states had a head start over the Davis government. As early as December, 1859, the Mississippi
legislature, in response to John Brown's raid at Harpers Ferry, had appropriated $150,000 for the pur-
chase of arms. By January, 1861, the Mississippians
had organized 65 companies of troops. "The military

fires enkindled within the chivalric sons of Mississippi within the past year," the state adjutant general then reported, "are unprecedented in her military annals." Mississippi and the other states, as they seceded, increased both their martial spirit and their military stores by the quick and easy conquest of Federal arsenals and forts. Florida and South Carolina, partially frustrated as they were, made their preparations with special vigor and eagerness. "Let us arm for the contest, and perhaps by a show of our force and our readiness for the combat we may escape the realities of war," Governor M. S. Perry of Florida proclaimed. "We have taken the field. Our flag is unfurled at Pensacola. . . ." The South Carolinians had been busy since December, 1860. "They are making every preparation (drilling nightly, &c.) for the fight which they say must take place, and insist on our not doing anything," as Major Anderson noted at that time. They were ready before Davis was, and their governor appealed to him for authorization to strike.

"The President shares the feeling expressed by you that Fort Sumter should be in our possession at the earliest possible moment," Secretary Walker replied to Governor Pickens (March 1). But that moment had not yet arrived. "Thorough preparation must be made before an attack is attempted, for the first blow must be successful. . . . A failure would demoralize our people and injuriously affect us in the opinion of the world as reckless and precipitate." Walker also informed Pickens that, in accordance with a resolution of Congress, the President was assuming control of all "military operations" in South Carolina and was appointing General P. G. T. Beauregard to take command of Charleston Harbor.

From Beauregard, after his arrival in Charleston, Walker and Davis learned that he was going to extend the harbor works so as to make the fort the center of a circle of firepower. "If Sumter was properly garrisoned and armed," Beauregard explained, it would be a perfect Gibraltar to anything but constant shelling, night and day, from the four points of the compass. As it is, the weakness of the garrison constitutes our greatest advantage, and we must, for the present, turn our attention to preventing it from being re-inforced."

In communicating the "negotiation or force" resolution to the Florida governor, Davis pointed out that Congress did not intend the efforts at negotiation to interfere with the preparations for force. The governor should therefore continue with "the instruction of troops, or other preparation, which will be useful in further operations." To take command at Pensacola, Davis appointed General Braxton Bragg. Soon Bragg issued an order forbidding all traffic between Pensacola and Fort Pickens. Troops continued to arrive and add to the build-up for the eventual assault. "Mobile looks more like a military barracks than a commercial city," Howell Cobb wrote to his wife on March 31. "There are some fifteen hundred troops here on their way to Pensacola—most of them from

Mississippi and composed of the best young men of the State."

As a military planner, Davis looked beyond the immediate tasks at Charleston and Pensacola. He took steps to secure more war material than could be used at those places. He sent an agent to the North to buy arms, ammunition, and machinery. He sent another agent to Europe not only to take what military goods were available on the market but also to make contracts for purchasing additional amounts to be manufactured in the future.

While thus preparing to use force, Davis also made the most he could out of the policy of negotiation. He followed the reports of the three commissioners in Washington—Martin J. Crawford, John Forsyth, and A. B. Roman—whom he had appointed on February 27. They told how, in their first interchanges with Seward, they had threatened immediate action to take the forts but (on March 8) had offered to wait twenty days before pressing the Confederate demands, provided Seward would promise that the military situation would remain unchanged. When Seward stalled, they decided to play along with him. "We are playing a game in which time is our best advocate, and if our Government could afford the time I feel confident of winning," Forsyth wrote to Walker (March 14). "Lincoln inclines to peace. . . . Since the 4th of March two of the Republican illusions have exploded—first, that it was very easy to reenforce the forts, and second, that they could collect the revenue on floating custom-houses at sea." A little more time, presumably, would explode other Republican illusions and would bring Lincoln, at last, to the realization that he must recognize the Confederacy.

Davis was willing to go along with the waiting policy of his commissioners, but not to accept the hints of conciliation that Seward emitted to them and to others. "Give but little credit to the rumors of an amicable adjustment," Davis had his war secretary warn Beauregard at Charleston. "Do not slacken for a moment your energies, and be ready to execute any order this Department may forward."

The commissioners thought it a good idea to go on waiting even when their twenty-day deadline had passed, and they considered it a great diplomatic victory for the Confederacy when Seward finally promised that his government would not, without notice, undertake to change the situation at Sumter. As Commissioner Crawford pointed out to Secretary Toombs, the Confederate States "were not bound in any way whatever to observe the same course" toward the United States (but were left free to strike at Sumter without warning). "We think, then," Crawford said, "that the policy of 'masterly inactivity,' on our part, was wise in every particular."

Davis and Toombs agreed with the commissioners. Toombs instructed them to maintain their present position and make no demand for an official hearing or an official answer. It was well that, for the time being, the United States should neither declare war nor arrange peace. "It affords the Confederate States the advantages of both conditions, and enables them to make all the necessary arrangements for the public defense, and the solidifying of their Government, more safely, more cheaply, and expeditiously than they would were the attitude of the United States more definite and decided."

From the Confederate point of view, at the beginning of April, the policy of Davis seemed to have worked quite well, indeed. He was far readier for military action than Lincoln was. He had more armed men at his call than Lincoln did. There were four or five thousand at Pensacola, five or six thousand at Charleston. At Charleston the Confederates had the better guns and the better emplacements.

And Beauregard was all set, almost, to use them. He had advised the Davis government (March 27) that the expulsion of Anderson from Fort Sumter "ought now to be decided on in a few days, for this state of uncertainty ought not to last longer than is necessary to have all our preparations made to compel him to a surrender, should the United States Government not be willing to withdraw him peaceably."

It was a matter of time, and by now the time had nearly arrived for abandoning negotiation and concentrating upon force—even though Lincoln should do no more than keep on refusing to yield the forts.[3]

4

IN the Government House, on April 2, Davis and Walker prepared a reply to Beauregard, who had sent them a copy of a telegram he had received from Commissioner Crawford. The Commissioner, relaying the information that the Lincoln government would not undertake to supply Sumter without notice, assumed (mistakenly, of course) that the majority of Lincoln's cabinet still favored evacuating Sumter. "My opinion is that the President has not the courage to execute the order agreed upon in Cabinet for the evacuation of the fort, but that he intends to shift the responsibility upon Major Anderson, by suffering him to be starved out," Crawford said. "Would it not be well to aid in this by cutting off all supplies?"

Up to this time, though Anderson was running short of staple provisions and other necessaries, he had been permitted to buy fresh groceries and meats in Charleston. It would be foolish to go on allowing him to do so—if it were true that Lincoln now was sitting back, shrinking from action, and passing the buck to Anderson.

"Batteries here ready to open Wednesday or Thursday [April 4 or 5]," Beauregard added, on his own. "What instructions?"

The following reply, with Walker's signature, went on April 2 from Davis to Beauregard:

"The Government [at Montgomery] has at no time placed any reliance on assurances by the Government at Washington in respect to the evacuation of Fort Sumter, or entertained any confidence in the disposition of the latter to make any concession or yield any point to which it is not driven by absolute necessity, and I desire that you govern yourself with strict reference to this as the key to the policy of the Confederate States.

"You are especially instructed to remit in no degree your efforts to prevent the re-enforcement of Fort Sumter, and to keep yourself in a state of the amplest preparation and most perfect readiness to repel invasion—save only in commencing an assault or attack, except to repel an invading or re-enforcing force—precisely as if you were in the presence of an enemy contemplating to surprise you.

"The delays and apparent vacillation of the Washington Government make it imperative that the further concession of courtesies . . . to Major Anderson . . . in supplies from the city, must cease. . . .

"Until the withdrawal of the Commissioners . . . from Washington—an event which may occur at any moment—no operations beyond what is indicated in the foregoing would be permissible. Promptly, however, on the receipt by this Government of the intelligence of such withdrawal the Department will transmit to you specific instructions for your guidance."

These instructions from Davis to Beauregard were

firm and clear. Do not expect Lincoln voluntarily to abandon the fort. Put yourself on a war footing, but do not strike yet, except to repel an enemy expedition. Cut off Anderson's food purchases in Charleston. Be ready for additional orders whenever the news comes that the Confederate diplomats in Washington have terminated their mission. Their departure, probably, will be the signal for you to open fire.

During the next week, however, reports from Crawford, Forsyth, and Roman indicated that the time for action might arrive even before these men left Washington. From them the Montgomery government received a flurry of telegrams, full of changing and confusing rumors: Lincoln has been conferring with naval engineers, perhaps in regard to reinforcing the fort at Charleston, perhaps in regard to collecting the revenue at New Orleans. Much activity in the War and Navy departments. The *Powhatan* is being put in commission to sail. It is said that these movements have reference to "the San Domingo question." More activity, more movements. "The statement that this armament is intended for St. Domingo may be a mere ruse." No letup in the warlike preparations. "The rumor that they are destined against Pickens and perhaps Sumter is getting every day stronger." "We have not yet been notified of the movement, but the notification may come when they are ready to start." "Watch at all points."

Then, on April 8, the Montgomery government learned and promptly informed Bragg and Beauregard: "Our Commissioners at Washington have received a flat refusal."

Now, at last, all the talk about negotiation was finished. The diplomats would be departing soon. The time for the soldiers to act was at hand.

Davis immediately had letters sent out to the seven governors, asking them to raise a total of 20,000 additional troops. "The discontinuance by the United States of negotiations with the Commissioners representing this Government," the letters said, "leaves no doubt as to the policy we should pursue."

That night, April 8, another telegram arrived from Charleston. In it Beauregard said: "Authorized messenger from Lincoln just informed Governor Pickens and myself that provisions would be sent to Sumter peaceably, otherwise by force." (Beauregard neglected to send along a copy of the actual text of Lincoln's notice.)

The men in Montgomery took little time to reflect upon Beauregard's report. Their reply was almost automatic. They were now aware that *provisions* were being sent, and "peaceably" if possible. But already, before getting this news, they had had no doubt as to the policy they should pursue.

That same night Walker, on behalf of Davis, wired back to Beauregard: "Under no circumstances are you to allow provisions to be sent to Fort Sumter."[4]

5

DAVIS might have left it at that—
with instructions for Beauregard to wait until the Sumter expedition approached and then resist the provisioning attempt. To wait, to react only in the face of provocation and directly against the provoking force, would perhaps have the advantage of showing the world that the United States was actually making the aggressive move and the Confederate States only taking a defensive stand.

Or Davis might have reconsidered those instructions and sent new ones—to let food be landed but not arms or men. He knew that Fort Sumter posed no actual, physical threat to the people of Charleston, for they were beyond the reach of its guns. Months earlier, in January, he had counseled Governor Pickens to let the fort alone, writing: "The little garrison in its present position presses on nothing but a point of pride." The mere feeding of those hundred-odd men would not change the balance—or, rather, the imbalance—of the forces opposed to one another in Charleston Harbor.

That is to say, Davis might have postponed a resort to arms. He might, at the very least, have delayed long enough to let the other side, the approaching warships or the fort itself, begin the actual firing. "He has achieved his reputation as a soldier, and we are sure he feels no desire to augment a fame that might content any man, by civil war," the *New Orleans Picayune* had said. "He will have much to do to restrain the eagerness of the young soldier, who is panting to flash his maiden sword upon his country's enemies. He will have something to do to restrain the rashness of the misguided enthusiast, who requires the bonds of [Southern] union to be cemented in blood." Go slow! Be patient! the *Picayune* advised. "Would a little patience be more hurtful to us than the reputation of having struck the first blow?"

And the war, if one should begin, might not go quite so well for the Confederacy as many of its patriots expected. War might destroy the very thing the Confederacy had been designed to safeguard, that is, slavery. "The whole world outside the slaveholding States, with slight exceptions, is opposed to slavery; and the whole world, with slave labor thus rendered insecure and comparatively valueless, will take sides with the North against us," the *North Carolina Standard* of Raleigh had predicted. "The end will be—*Abolition!*" Davis himself sensed the probability of slavery's doom. "In any case," he had written to his wife, "I think our slave property will be lost eventually."

But Davis could only move ahead: he could not back up. He had too many panting soldiers to think of, too many blood-minded enthusiasts to take into account. If he should retreat, the Confederacy would have little chance to grow or even to live. His own position of leadership would be imperiled. The hot-headed Carolinians might take the initiative from him. They might begin the firing at any moment, regardless of instructions from Montgomery.

So Davis did not consider reversing himself when he met with his cabinet for lengthy consultations on April 9 and 10. The only questions he and his advisers really entertained were these: Could they be sure the notice to Governor Pickens was genuine? If so, should they content themselves with the orders already given to Beauregard, or should they instruct him to act immediately? That is, should they have Beauregard open fire *before*, rather than after, the arrival of Lincoln's expedition? It was an issue of timing.

In the midst of the cabinet discussions, on April 10, Davis received a rather long telegram from his old friend Senator Louis Wigfall, of Texas. Wigfall was now in Charleston. His telegram read: "No one doubts that Lincoln intends war. The delay on his part is only to complete his preparations. All here is ready on our side. Our delay therefore is to his advantage, and our disadvantage. Let us take Fort Sumter before we have to fight the fleet and the fort. General Beauregard will not act without your order. Let me suggest to you to send the order to him to begin the attack as soon as he is ready. Virginia is excited by the preparations, and a bold stroke on our side will complete her purposes. Policy and prudence are urgent upon us to begin at once."

Later in the day Davis, through Walker, telegraphed to Beauregard: "If you have no doubt of the authorized character of the agent who communicated to you the intention of the Washington Government to supply Fort Sumter by force you will at once demand its evacuation, and if this is refused proceed, in such manner as you may determine, to reduce it. Answer."

Beauregard answered that the demand would be made at noon the next day. Walker wired back to insist that, unless there were "special reasons," Beauregard should make the demand before that time. Davis, it appeared, was now in a hurry.

The next day, April 11, there was another interchange of telegrams, several of them, between Beauregard and Walker. Beauregard, as he reported, did not present the demand until two in the afternoon and did not require a reply until six. (Anderson was an old friend of his and once had taught him at West Point.) That evening, as Beauregard reported again, Anderson presented a written rejection but, in doing so, remarked that if the fort was not battered to pieces around them, he and his men would be starved out in a few days. Davis and Walker discussed Anderson's response. Then Walker wired to Beauregard that the government did not wish to start a needless bombardment, that Beauregard might "avoid the effusion of blood" if Anderson would state a definite time for evacuation and would withhold fire until then. "If this or its equivalent be refused," Walker told Beauregard, "reduce the fort as your judgment decides to be most practicable."

After an anxious night for Davis and his colleagues, Walker telegraphed to Beauregard the next morning, April 12: "What was Major Anderson's reply to the proposition contained in my despatch of last night?"

The anxiety was lessened a little when the mail brought a fat envelope from Governor Pickens. No longer could there be the slightest doubt that the recent notice to the governor, purportedly from Lincoln, veritably had come from him. Here was proof. Governor Pickens enclosed letters which Anderson had dispatched for Washington but which the Confederate authorities had seized. In one of these letters, from Anderson to his superiors in Washington, he acknowledged receipt of the communication, dated April 4, telling him that an expedition was on the way to Sumter.

(It was just as well, for Anderson's reputation in the North, that this letter did not get to Washington. In it Anderson expressed surprise and chagrin. He predicted "most disastrous results" throughout the country. He went so far as to say: "My heart is not in the war which I see is to be thus commenced." So wrote the man whom Northerners soon were to hail as the hero of the war's first battle!)

Preoccupied as they were with Fort Sumter, Davis and his advisers almost forgot, for the nonce, about Fort Pickens. Suddenly they were reminded. On April 12 they got word that a United States naval officer was on the way to Pensacola with dispatches. "Intercept them," Walker quickly instructed Bragg by wire. But it was too late. "Alarm guns have just fired at Fort Pickens," Bragg telegraphed back. "I fear the news is received and it will be re-enforced before morning. It cannot be prevented."

Better tidings came that day from Charleston. Anderson's last reply had been unsatisfactory. The Confederate guns had opened. Fort Sumter was being pounded. It would be neither provisioned nor reinforced.[5]

6. Consequences

1

"EXTRY! EXTRY!" newsboys were shouting on the streets of New York. "Bombardment of Fort Sumter!" One businessman, out for an evening stroll with friends, at first refused to buy a paper: he thought the vendors' cry a mere "sell." For days there had been reports—false, as they turned out—of firing on the fort. After walking about four blocks, though, the man gave in, bought a paper, and, by the light of a corner gas lamp, read it to his companions. The dispatch about Sumter sounded genuine, yet this reader still found it difficult to believe. "I can hardly hope," he said, "that the rebels have been so foolish and thoughtless as to take the initiative in civil war and bring matters to a crisis. If so, they have put themselves in a horribly false position. The most frantic Virginian can hardly assert that this war is brought on by an attempt at 'coercion.'"

In Washington the next morning, April 13, Lincoln was ready with a statement for the frantic Virginians. Three of them, delegates from the Virginia convention, were coming to get his response to the convention's resolution of April 8. This resolution, declaring that the uncertainty with regard to his intentions was itself a threat to peace, requested the President to inform the convention what policy he was going to pursue.

In the answer he had drafted, Lincoln said it was "with deep regret, and some mortification," he had learned there was "great, and injurious uncertainty, in the public mind." For he was still following the very same course he had marked out in his inaugural address. He would now repeat: "The power confided to me will be used to hold, occupy, and possess, the property, and places belonging to the Government, and to collect the duties, and imposts; but, beyond what is necessary for these objects, there will be no invasion —no using of force against, or among the people anywhere." By the words "property, and places, belonging to the Government," he had meant "chiefly" the military posts actually in the possession of the government at the time he took office.

"But"—the draft continued—"if, by efforts to drive the United States forces from these places, either by assault or starvation, a collision of arms shall be occasioned, I shall hold myself at liberty to re-possess, if I can, like places which had been seized before the Government was devolved upon me."

Since penning that sentence, Lincoln had received additional news from Charleston, and so, before the committee of three Virginians appeared at the White House, he revised the passage to read: "But if, as now appears to be true, in pursuit of a purpose to drive the United States authority from these places, an unprovoked assault has been made at Fort-Sumter, I shall hold myself at liberty," etc.

That is, Lincoln now was saying, he intended to enlarge somewhat the policy which, up to this time, he had been following. Certainly, he would "repel force by force." Perhaps he would withdraw the Federal mail service from the states that claimed to have seceded—"believing that the commencement of actual war against the Government justifies and possibly demands this." Yet he would not go so far as to wage actual war, general war, on his own part. "Whatever else I may do for the purpose, I shall not attempt to collect the duties, and imposts, by any armed invasion of any part of the country—not meaning by this, however, that I may not land a force, deemed necessary, to relieve a fort upon a border of the country."

This statement, as he had revised it, Lincoln read to the three Virginians when they arrived for their answer on that Saturday morning.

On Sunday morning, April 14, Lincoln met with his cabinet. According to the late news, Major Anderson this day was evacuating Sumter; he had agreed the previous day to surrender. The cabinet discussed the question what to do next. Sooner or later, military and naval forces would have to be gathered for retaking Sumter and the other forts, at least those forts which were accessible on the borders of the country. More immediately, additional troops would be needed to safeguard the capital, which appeared to be in worse danger than ever, even though Lincoln already had directed General Scott to muster into the service of the United States about fifteen companies of District of Columbia militia. Congress would have to be called into special session, in order to appropriate funds and take other necessary measures, but Congress must not assemble until the safety of the city had been reasonably well assured.

In the interim Lincoln would have to have some kind of legal authority on which to base military action. He and his advisers found such authority in a long-forgotten law of 1795 which gave the President the right, in certain circumstances, to call the state militia into Federal service. Following closely the wording of that law, he wrote out the draft of a presidential proclamation. This asked the governors of the non-seceded states for a total of 75,000 men, for three months, to put down "combinations" in seven states "too powerful to be suppressed by the ordinary course of judicial proceedings." The proclamation also summoned Congress for a special session to begin in about three months, on an appropriately patriotic day, the Fourth of July.

Later on Sunday, after putting the finishing touches on the proclamation, Lincoln welcomed a White House visitor, his old acquaintance and old antagonist Stephen A. Douglas. Quietly, confidentially, the two men talked at some length. Before Douglas left, Lincoln knew that, in the trying times ahead, he would have his full support.

On Monday morning, April 15, the proclamation calling for 75,000 troops was officially issued. It went out by telegraph from Washington, to be published the same day in newspapers throughout the country.

That day the cabinet met again, to talk further about strategy for dealing with the rebellion. Already, in his statement to the Virginia delegates, Lincoln had adumbrated a plan for strictly limited warfare. This plan ruled out all thought of an invasion, of an overland campaign against the revolted states. It did not, however, rule out the possibility of landings here and there along the coast, to recapture fortresses. Nor did it exclude the use of seapower for the offshore collection of customs or various measures of boycott, such as the mild one of withholding the mails. Now the cabinet considered other possible steps as well. The Southern ports might be closed. The Mississippi River might be sealed off, its navigation denied to the rebels.

"The plan of practically closing the ports of the insurgent States and cutting off all their Sea-ward commerce seems to me the cheapest and most humane method of restraining those States and destroying their Confederation," Attorney General Bates said, reading from a memorandum he had prepared. This plan "would not necessarily lead to the shedding of a drop of blood," and yet it would be "very promising of success." Bates continued: "Others may think it wiser and better to adopt a line of action more bold and warlike, and to enforce the laws at the point of the bayonet, in the field. If that opinion prevail then I have a suggestion to make." The suggestion was to "take and hold with strong hand the City of New Orleans." That could be done "without much fighting." A naval force could simply push upriver from the Gulf of Mexico while another force of eight or ten thousand boatmen ran down from Cairo. "I do not propose this plan," Bates made clear, "for I greatly prefer to accomplish the end by blockade."

In any case, the cabinet on April 15 had to concern itself more with defensive than with offensive planning. Most urgent was the need to protect St. Louis, Harpers Ferry, the Gosport Navy Yard at Norfolk, the Chesapeake and other approaches to Washington, and above all the capital itself. This need became obvious from the response that recent events were evoking in Virginia and in the states farther south.[1]

2

TO LINCOLN, the response throughout the North was gratifying enough. It was all that his informants, such as Carl Schurz, had led him to expect. The flag having been fired upon, men were eager to heed the President's call for troops, and women eager to see their sons, husbands, or sweethearts go to save the country. These enthusiasts included Democrats as well as Republicans, for suddenly the issue had become one of patriotism, not partisanship. The Democratic leader Douglas, on his way homeward from Washington to Illinois, declared for all to hear: "Every man must be for the United States or against it; there can be no neutrals in this war—only patriots and traitors."

The trend of opinion in New York City exemplified the trend in all the free states. "The Northern backbone is much stiffened already," an observant New Yorker wrote on April 13. "Many who stood up for 'Southern rights' and complained of wrongs done the South now say that, since the South has fired the first gun, they are ready to go all lengths in supporting the President." When the presidential proclamation was published, on April 15, the *New York Herald* began to switch from praise of Jefferson Davis to praise of Lincoln. Even Mayor Wood, who had been talking of secession for the city, changed his tune: he now urged all citizens to obey the laws of the land.

The reaction in the Confederate states, if far less gratifying to Lincoln, was equally enthusiastic. It paralleled, in reverse, the reaction in the free states. Men and women everywhere rejoiced, and men pledged to die, if need be, for the Confederate cause. The spirit of celebration culminated in Montgomery. Bonfires blazed on capitol hill, and in the yellow glare a band serenaded the officers of government. Responding, War Secretary Walker assured an excited crowd that the flag now flying over the Government House in Montgomery would, in less than a month, be flying also over the public buildings in Washington.

"We are prepared to fight, and the enemy is not," said the *Mobile Advertiser,* taking up the War Secretary's theme. "Now is the time for action, while he is yet unprepared. Let . . . a hundred thousand men . . .

get over the border as quickly as they can. Let a division enter every Northern border State, destroy railroad connections to prevent concentration of the enemy, and the desperate strait of these States, the body of Lincoln's country, will compel him to a peace —or compel his successor, should Virginia not suffer him to escape from his doomed capital."

There were a few dissenting voices in the Confederacy. In Charleston the fanatical Rhett, consistent in his fanaticism, continued for a while to argue that, once Virginia had seceded, war would be unnecessary. The Confederacy, enlarged by the accession of the other slave states, could command peace without striking another blow. For the time being, therefore, Rhett through the *Charleston Mercury* declared that the South stood upon the defensive, and he deprecated the popular talk of an immediate march upon Washington.

What would the Virginians do? For Lincoln, as for many others, North and South, that was the big question. The *New York Herald*, on April 13, printed a Charleston dispatch which said that the venerable Edmund Ruffin, one of those Virginia agitators in Charleston, personally had touched off the first cannon to fire a ball at Sumter. "That ball," the Charleston source stated, "will do more for the cause of secession in Virginia than volumes of stump speeches." Still, as late as April 16, the *New York Herald* and other Northern papers predicted that Lincoln's firm policy would stifle rebellion in Virginia and all the border states.

Events soon belied the hopes and confirmed the fears of Lincoln and the North. By the time his call for

·161·

troops was reported in Richmond, on the evening of April 15, that city already was full of secessionists from all parts of the state. These men were on hand to take part in a "Spontaneous Southern Rights" assembly, which in fact was anything but spontaneous, having been carefully planned by leaders impatient with the existing convention and with Governor Robert Letcher. The secessionists, in and out of the convention, were conspiring to seize control of the state, depose the Governor, and join the Confederacy. They were all set for a coup when the news of Lincoln's call arrived. This news saved Virginia from a possible revolution, for it convinced the majority of Virginians that Lincoln was about to make war, illegally and unconstitutionally, and that they had no choice but to fight on the side of the South.

On April 17 the Virginia convention adopted an ordinance of secession.

On the same day, from Montgomery, Jefferson Davis responded to Lincoln's proclamation with a proclamation of his own. This amounted to a Confederate declaration of war. In it Davis averred that the President of the United States had "announced his intention of invading the Confederacy with an armed force, for the purpose of capturing its fortresses, and thereby subverting its independence and subjecting the free people thereof to the dominion of a foreign power." Therefore, Davis went on, it had become the duty of his government "to repel the threatened invasion, and defend the rights and liberties of the people by all the means which the laws of nations and usages of civilized warfare place at its disposal." Getting down to specific means of warfare, Davis offered letters of marque and reprisal to the armed privateers of any nationality willing to accept his invitation to prey upon the seaborne commerce of the United States.[2]

3

FOR the next week Lincoln wondered from day to day how long the city of Washington could hold out. One afternoon, sitting alone in his office, he felt a sense of utter desertion and helplessness. It occurred to him that a fair-sized body of secessionist troops, if they happened to be in the vicinity, could easily march over the Long Bridge across the Potomac and capture him and his cabinet. As he was musing he suddenly thought he heard the boom of a cannon in the distance. He got up and went out of the room to see what was going on, but no one else in the White House had heard any unusual sound. He must have been hearing things.

But the capital was in danger: he was not merely imagining that. Guarding the city were a few marines, six companies of the regular army, and fifteen companies of inexperienced volunteers. To supplement those thin forces, some three or four hundred Pennsylvania militiamen arrived, without sufficient arms and equipment, on the evening of April 18. Impatiently, Lincoln waited for the arrival of more men and more arms from the North. The troops on hand were far too few to save the city from the tide of secessionism that threatened to engulf it.

The Confederates were proceeding as if to make good their boast that Washington soon would be theirs. They held the initiative in the fast-broadening hostilities. They had loosed upon Northern shipping the pirates of the world, or at least had undertaken to do so. They had gained the support of Virginia and, it appeared, were about to gain the support of Maryland. The embattled Virginians, the day after seceding, took the Federal arsenal at Harpers Ferry and, two days after that, the Federal navy yard at Norfolk. The most the Union forces had been able to do, before retreating from those two places, was to burn or otherwise destroy most of the war material. Meanwhile, on April 19, the rebellious Marylanders rose up.

On that day, amid the succession of disasters for the Union cause, Lincoln issued a second proclamation, this one a reply to Davis' recent proclamation offering commissions to Confederate privateers. Lincoln now announced that he would set on foot a blockade of the insurgent ports and that he would hold Davis' privateers "amenable to the laws of the United States for the prevention and punishment of piracy." That is, he would see that the privateering officers and crews were hanged, once they had been captured and convicted. Though he did not so intend it, the proclamation of blockade was, in effect, a declaration of hostilities on the part of the United States (and the Supreme Court later was to take this proclamation as marking, from the legal point of view, the onset of the Civil War). At the moment, it was only a statement of intent and, considering the plight of the United States government, a rather desperate statement at that.

For, on the same day, occurred the Baltimore riot. Many Baltimoreans, including city officials, though not the mayor, were determined secessionists, and so were most members of the Maryland legislature. In the city, and in the counties adjacent to Washington, there was a secret organization with the ultimate aim of seizing the national capital and setting up a provisional government to serve the interests of the Confederacy. On April 19, however, the immediate objective of the Maryland secessionists was to prevent the relief of Washington by Northern troops. Rioters set upon the Sixth Regiment of Massachusetts Volunteers as the soldiers were on their way through Baltimore. Four of the soldiers were killed and about thirty wounded (and two or three times as many Baltimoreans).

Immediately the Baltimore conspirators sent to Richmond for a supply of arms. Responding with alacrity, the Virginia governor forwarded two thousand muskets and promised twenty heavy guns. President Davis encouraged Governor Letcher. "Sustain Baltimore, if practicable," Davis telegraphed to him. "We reinforce you." And Davis ordered thirteen regiments of Confederate troops to concentrate in Virginia and reinforce the governor in his efforts to sustain Baltimore. With Baltimore as well as Harpers Ferry in secessionist control, Davis would practically have succeeded in encircling and isolating the District of Columbia.

For a few days the Confederate chances looked good, the Union prospects bad. Marylanders destroyed the railroad bridges connecting Baltimore with the North. The Maryland governor, Thomas Hicks, wired Lincoln: "Send no more troops here." Lincoln, in his extremity, requested an interview with the Governor and the Mayor. The Governor being ill, the Mayor came with three prominent citizens of Baltimore, on April 21. Lincoln told them that the Northern troops were intended not for aggression against the South but for the protection of Washington, and they must be given safe transit through Maryland. They would not have to use the Baltimore streets: they could take wagon roads around the city, or they could come by Chesapeake Bay and through Annapolis. The Mayor assured Lincoln that the city authorities would do their best to prevent interference with these roundabout routes.

Though the men of the Sixth Massachusetts had reached Washington, after fighting their way through Baltimore, Lincoln still had doubts about the capital's safety when, on April 24, he was invited to talk peace. The invitation came from Minister Schleiden, of Bremen, whom Secretary Seward had brought to the White House. The city of Bremen was much interested in American trade, and Schleiden hoped to prevent its disruption by preventing civil war. He offered to go to Richmond, see Alexander H. Stephens, who was there, and find out the terms on which the Confederates would consider an armistice.

Lincoln thanked Schleiden for his willingness to help in avoiding bloodshed. He said he rather wished

Schleiden had gone ahead, on his own, without consulting the President or the Secretary of State. Schleiden protested that, if he had done so, he would have laid himself open to the suspicion of intriguing with the rebels against the legitimate government. Lincoln agreed. He went on to say he favored peace, but his official statements on the subject had been misinterpreted, had given rise to charges of imbecility and cowardice, and so he had resolved not to make any new statements on the subject. He added that he did not have in mind any aggression against the Southern states but only the safety of the government and the capital—and "the possibility to govern everywhere" throughout the land. Though he could neither authorize negotiations nor invite proposals, he promised to consider carefully any proposal which Schleiden might find himself called upon to submit.

On April 25 two more Northern regiments arrived, the Eighth Massachusetts and the Seventh New York. As they marched up Pennsylvania Avenue, about noon, with bands playing and banners flying, they dispelled most of the gloom and doubt and fear that had been hanging over Washington. Lincoln came out to wave at the men as they passed the White House. He looked like the happiest person in town: he "smiled all over," it seemed to one man who watched him.

On the train bringing the troops from Annapolis had come Carl Schurz, now the minister-elect to Spain. Calling at the White House, Schurz told Lincoln he would like to give up the Spanish mission, remain in the United States, and begin at once to raise a cavalry force of German-Americans. Lincoln advised him not to be so hasty. The war, if there was to be one, might not last long, he explained. Many people thought it would not. Seward was speaking of sixty to ninety days. He himself was not quite so optimistic as that. Still, he might be wrong. He could tell better in a few weeks.

The very next day, however, Lincoln indicated that he was taking no chances, even though he could not yet foresee how serious or prolonged the struggle might become. Heretofore he had been receiving troops who, in response to his call, had volunteered to serve for three months. Henceforth he would receive only those who volunteered for three years. So, on April 26, the New Jersey governor was informed. A three-year war, perhaps.

A day or two later Lincoln heard again from the aspiring peacemaker Schleiden. The man had gathered, from his recent conversation at the White House, that Lincoln wanted him to go unofficially to Richmond and talk with Stephens. Seward, urging him on, had given him a pass through the Union lines. Schleiden had gone. He now sent Lincoln a report, including letters from Stephens.

Schleiden had proposed to Stephens that Davis' proclamation on privateering and Lincoln's on the blockade be simultaneously revoked, and that all hostilities be suspended for a period of three months. Stephens, however, favored a "de facto truce through tactful avoidance of attack on both sides," rather than a formal armistice. Neither Montgomery nor Richmond, he said, contemplated an attack upon Washington, but it was a necessary condition of peace that Maryland be allowed to join the Confederacy. A further condition was that Lincoln should recommend to Congress, when it assembled on July 4, the propriety of treating with the Confederate commissioners and negotiating an amicable settlement of differences outstanding between the two countries. Stephens thought it futile to hope that Lincoln and the Republicans would agree. "It seems to be their policy to wage a war for the recapture of former possessions, looking to the ultimate coercion and subjugation of the people of the Confederate States to their power and domain," Stephens explained. "With such an object on their part persevered in, no power on earth can arrest or prevent a most bloody conflict."

This made it clear to Lincoln, if he still had the slightest doubt, that no peace was possible without disunion. He gave Seward an unofficial and confidential message for the well-meaning Schleiden. The gist of it was that there was no point in going on with the negotiations.[3]

4

ONLY about two weeks had gone by since April 12, but in those two weeks so much had happened that, to Lincoln, the Sumter and Pickens expeditions now seemed remote, almost like topics from ancient history.

The history of Fort Pickens, in its climactic chapter, was most gratifying to all the Union men who had a part in the events. On April 12 the overland messenger from Washington, Lieutenant Worden, managed to get a boat in Pensacola to take him out in the harbor to the ship of Captain Adams, the naval officer in command of the Union squadron, who previously had questioned the order from General Scott to land the reinforcing troops already present on shipboard. Worden delivered, from memory, the new order from Secretary Welles. That night, under the cover of darkness, the waiting soldiers and marines made their way into the fort. There was no opposition, no sign that the rebels even knew what was going on. A few days later the *Atlantic* arrived with additional men, and on April 17 the *Powhatan* steamed in, flying the British flag as a *ruse de guerre*. Pickens was safe.

Quite different was the history of Fort Sumter. The fate of the Sumter expedition was far from gratifying to the man most intimately concerned with the venture, Gustavus Vasa Fox. He was filled with a sense of failure and humiliation. Returning northward aboard the *Baltic*, bringing with him Major Anderson and the veterans of the surrendered garrison, Fox told his story and poured out his feelings in page after page which he wrote, in pencil, to his sponsor, friend, and brother-in-law Montgomery Blair.

At three o'clock on the morning of April 12, after three days of bad weather and heavy sea, Fox and his transport, the *Baltic*, had finally reached the rendezvous ten miles east of the Charleston light. There he found only the revenue cutter *Harriet Lane* awaiting him. A few hours later the warship *Pawnee* appeared, but the *Pocahontas,* the *Powhatan,* and the tugs were nowhere to be seen. With neither the tugs nor the *Powhatan's* sailors, Fox lacked the means to make a serious provisioning attempt. Nevertheless, he decided to do what he could. Then, as he started to steam in toward the harbor, he became aware that Sumter and the batteries around it already were engaged in a furious cannonade.

He consulted with the commanders of the *Pawnee* and the *Harriet Lane.* He thought an attempt should be made, as soon as night fell, to run in the few boats they could man. The others pointed out that they had orders to wait for the *Powhatan's* arrival. They promised, however, that they would co-operate in an effort the next morning, whether the *Powhatan* had appeared or not. That night Fox watched for her in vain. "It blew very heavy all night with a great swell and towards morning a thick fog." In the morning the waves were so high it was impossible to load the boats. And now thick clouds of black smoke began to rise from Fort Sumter while Fox looked on, helpless and horrified. "The barbarians, to their everlasting disgrace be it said, redoubled their fire, and through the flames and smoke the noble band of true men continued their response."

Not till this day did Fox learn, from the *Pawnee's* captain, that the *Powhatan* was not coming at all, that she had been detached for duty elsewhere. (Why the captain had not told him earlier, Fox failed to explain.)

Despite this disillusionment, he determined upon a final, desperate plan. Once the sea had calmed and darkness had come, he would go in with provisions and men in an ice schooner which the *Pawnee* had seized. But that afternoon, just after the *Pocahontas* at last hove to, the fort surrendered. At Fox's suggestion, a boat went in with a flag of truce to offer passage in his ship for Major Anderson and the gallant men. (None of them had been killed, though the fort was practically in ruins. The only death on either side occurred the next day when, in firing a salute at the evacuation ceremonies, one of the Sumter guns exploded and fatally injured a member of its crew.)

Anderson, when Fox greeted him, was not in a very friendly mood. He felt that the government had neglected him, had given him inadequate information. He thought that Fox should have spoken more fully and frankly to him at the time of Fox's Sumter visit in March. Now, as the two men traveled together on the northbound ship, Fox took pains to tell Anderson about Lincoln's policy and his own "delicacy" in carrying it out. "I told the Major how anxious the President was that they (S.C.) should stand before the civilized world as having fired upon bread, yet they had made the case much worse for themselves as they knew the Major would leave the 15th at noon for want of provisions (see his correspondence), yet they opened upon 60 men and continued it whilst the fort was burning." "I also explained the reasons for holding the fort, far superior to any military ones, and told the Major I thought the Government would feel particularly gratified at the result." Before long, Anderson seemed to be satisfied with the way he had been treated.

But Fox was far from satisfied with the way *he* had been. He remained bitter. Someone, by detaching the *Powhatan*, had contrived deliberately to "extinguish" the Sumter expedition, he was sure. "I do not think I have deserved this treatment, and at present will not speak as I have felt, and now feel." "Had the *Powhatan* arrived the 12th we should have had the men and provisions into Fort Sumpter, as I had everything ready, boats, muffled oars, small packages of provisions, in fact everything but the 300 sailors promised to me by the [Navy] Department." "I think the President will keenly approve the Major's course. As for our expedition, somebody's influence has made it ridiculous." Anderson would be the hero, and Fox would be the goat.

Replying to Fox from Washington, Blair tried to reassure him but refrained from discussing the "Fort Sumpter business," because it was "not agreeable" for him to do so, and because Fox would know what he thought, anyhow. Besides, there was much more important business afoot these days. "We are now fairly launched in a big war." Fox could have a part in it if he wished. On the day Lincoln issued his blockade proclamation, the cabinet had discussed a plan to convert merchant vessels into armed ships. "During the talk the President said he wanted you to have a command tho you did not get into Fort Sumpter. He thought very highly of you." Blair had shown one of Fox's letters to Seward and Welles. "Seward read a part of it and handed it back without remark. Welles said when he handed it back that you knew, he supposed, that he had nothing to do with the diversion of the *Powhatan* from her Charleston mission. But the President has never had an opportunity to read or talk about the affair, except on the occasion mentioned, and indeed events of such magnitude are crowding on us that Sumpter and Anderson are not thought of for the moment."

Before the end of April, Lincoln felt compelled to give some thought to Fort Sumter and to its frustrated savior. The fuming Fox was now in Washington, digging up "all particulars about the *Powhatan* and other matters." He gathered that Seward had got up the Pensacola expedition and that Lincoln had signed the orders for it without fully understanding all their implications. Lincoln saw Fox and talked consolingly to him. "The President offers every apology possible," Fox wrote to his wife, "and will do so in writing." True to his word, Lincoln on May 1 composed the following letter to Fox:

"I sincerely regret the failure of the late attempt to provision Fort Sumpter should be the source of any annoyance to you. The practicability of your plan was not, in fact, brought to a test. By reason of a gale, well known in advance to be possible, and not improbable, the tugs, an essential part of the plan, never reached the ground; while, by an accident, for which you were in no wise responsible, and possibly I to some extent was, you were deprived of a war vessel, with her men, which you deemed of great importance to the enterprize.

CONSEQUENCES

"I most cheerfully and truly declare that the failure of the undertaking has not lowered you a particle, while the qualities you developed in the effort have greatly heightened you in my estimation. For a daring and dangerous enterprize of a similar character, you would to-day be the man, of all my acquaintances, whom I would select.

"You and I both anticipated that the cause of the country would be advanced by making the attempt to provision Fort Sumpter, even if it should fail; and it is no small consolation now to feel that our anticipation is justified by the result."[4]

5

AS the Fourth of July approached, congressmen gathered in Washington, to contend with the summer heat, the swarms of mosquitoes, the stench of privies, and the holiday crowds with their fireworks. Lincoln was ready with a message in which he justified his Sumter policy, but few of the congressmen, the Washingtonians, or the Northern people as a whole looked forward with much interest to what the President was going to say. Most of them were more concerned with what he and Congress were going to do. By now, there was a war, a real war, to fight and win.

Lincoln himself no longer doubted this. He realized he could not put down the rebellion, as he once had hoped he could, by mild and more or less bloodless measures. He could not rely on blockade and boycott and an occasional seaborne campaign to retake one of the lost forts. Already a Union army, under General George B. McClellan, was fighting a campaign in western Virginia to clear the Confederate forces out of that border area. Another army, under General Irvin McDowell, was encamped in Virginia about twenty miles southwest of Washington (and was to take part in the war's first big battle, at Bull Run, in less than three weeks). These and yet more armies would be needed, judging by the signs of the times: the secession of Virginia and then of Arkansas, Tennessee, and North Carolina; the secessionist uprising in Maryland; the assertion of neutrality in Kentucky; the rebel resistance in Missouri; and the avowals of preparation and determination on the part of the revolutionary leaders in Montgomery.

Already (April 29) Jefferson Davis had convened his own Congress in special session, boasted of his readiness for battle, and presented a rationalization of the Confederate cause. He announced that he had "in the field at Charleston, Pensacola, Forts Morgan, Jackson, St. Philip, and Pulaski, nineteen thousand men," and en route to Virginia sixteen thousand more. He promised, in addition, to "organize and hold in readiness for instant action" an army of a hundred thousand. All these troops were necessary, he said, because hostilities had been forced upon the Confederacy: Lincoln's proclamation calling out the state militia was, though irregular and illegal, a "plain declaration of war."

War had come, according to Davis, in consequence of the Lincoln government's "crooked path of diplomacy." Lincoln and Seward had deceived the Confederate diplomats. "While the Commissioners were receiving assurances calculated to inspire hope in the success of their mission, the Secretary of State and the President of the United States had already determined to hold no intercourse with them whatever, to refuse even to listen to any proposals they had to make; and had profited by the delay created by their own assurances, in order to prepare secretly the means of effective hostile operations."

Davis conceded that the Lincoln administration had given notice of "its purpose to use force if opposed in its intention of supplying Fort Sumter." "Yet, with our commissioners actually in Washington, detained under assurances that notice would be given of any military movement, the notice was not addressed to *them*, but a messenger was sent to Charleston to give notice to the Governor of South Carolina, and the notice was so given at a late hour on the 8th of April, the eve of the very day on which the fleet might be expected to arrive. The fact that this manoeuvre failed in its purpose was not the fault of those who contrived it."

Apparently Davis was hard put to demonstrate his own innocence and Lincoln's guilt. He was being thoroughly disingenuous. Indeed, he seemed to be projecting upon Lincoln his own motives with respect to the commissioners and their diplomacy. *He*, not Lincoln, had intended thereby to gain time for military preparations. And the commissioners had supposed that *they* were deluding Seward, rather than the other way around.

Not many in the North were likely to be taken in by

the Southern case as Davis presented it. "The course actually pursued gives the lie to the unblushing assertion of Jefferson Davis and his supporters, that war has been forced upon them," the *Boston Advertiser* commented. "Peace and independence were within their reach, but not only did they at last open hostilities, but their whole course was such as to force the [United States] government finally to defend itself in arms. They had their choice between the quiet separation of seven States, or more extensive movements with the danger of war, and they deliberately chose the latter."

Nevertheless, Lincoln as well as Davis had much to explain and justify. Since April 12, he had suspended the writ of habeas corpus and resorted to martial law and arbitrary arrests in order to keep Maryland in the Union. Going beyond his call for state militia and for three-year volunteers, he had increased the size of the regular army. He would need congressional approval, retrospectively, for some of his actions; strictly speaking, he ought to have secured congressional approval in advance.

Lincoln would also need to say something, to Congress and the country, about what he had done with regard to Sumter. Before April 12, many Northerners and, indeed, many Republicans had urged half measures, had proposed that Fort Sumter be sacrificed and that Fort Pickens be held as an alternative symbol of the national authority. Though the popular response to the actual Sumter policy had been overwhelmingly favorable, there were Northerners who, even yet, questioned whether the Sumter expedition could not have been held back. For the record, and for the benefit of these lingering doubters in particular, it would be well for Lincoln to underline his unaggressive intent and his limited choice of alternatives. In rationalizing for the record, as he wrote out his message for the July 4 session of Congress, Lincoln could not quite remember, perhaps, exactly what his plans and purposes had been at various points of time between his inauguration and his final decision with regard to Sumter.

On the eve of Independence Day, Lincoln read to a friend the draft of his message to Congress. The friend was Orville H. Browning, the new senator from Illinois, replacing Stephen A. Douglas, whose untimely death had been a blow to Lincoln.

In the passages concerning his Sumter policy, Lincoln now related how, upon his taking office, he had been faced with the duty of preventing, if possible, the consummation of an attempt to "destroy the Federal Union." He had to make a choice of means, and he did so, announcing the choice in his inaugural address. "The policy chosen looked to the exhaustion of all peaceful measures, before a resort to any stronger ones," he explained in the congressional message, as Browning listened. "It sought only to hold the public places and property, not already wrested from the Government, and to collect the revenue; relying for the rest on time, discussion, and the ballot-box."

Then, on the day after his inauguration, Lincoln had learned of Sumter's predicament. He thought that to abandon the fort, under the circumstances, would be "utterly ruinous," for the *necessity* of doing so "would not be fully understood." He considered the Pickens alternative. "Starvation was not yet upon the [Sumter] garrison; and ere it would be reached, *Fort Pickens* might be reinforced. This last would be a clear indication of *policy*, and would enable the country to accept the evacuation of Fort Sumter, as a military *necessity.*" So an order was promptly sent for landing the troops who were already present on shipboard in Pensacola harbor. "The first return news from the order was received just one week before the fall of Fort Sumter." "To now re-inforce Fort Pickens, before a crisis would be reached at Fort Sumter, was impossible." "In precaution against such a conjuncture, the government had, a few days before, commenced preparing an expedition . . . to relieve Fort Sumter, which expedition was intended to be ultimately used, or not, according to circumstances. The strongest anticipated case, for using it, was now presented; and it was resolved to send it forward."

"This notice [to the governor of South Carolina] was accordingly given; whereupon the Fort was attacked, and bombarded to its fall, without even awaiting the arrival of the provisioning expedition. It is thus seen that the assault . . . was, in no sense, a matter of self-defence on the part of the assailants. . . . They knew—they were expressly notified—that the giving of bread to the few brave and hungry men of the garrison was all which would on that occasion be attempted, unless themselves, by resisting so much, should provoke more." The real object of the assailants was "to drive out the visible authority of the Federal Union, and thus force it to immediate dissolution."

"That this was their object, the Executive well understood; and having said to them in the inaugural address, 'You can have no conflict without being yourselves the aggressors,' he took pains, not only to keep this declaration good, but also to keep the case so free from the power of ingenious sophistry, as that the world should not be able to misunderstand it. By the affair at Fort Sumter, with its surrounding circumstances, that point was reached. Then, and thereby, the assailants of the Government began the conflict of arms. . . ."

Having read these passages to his friend Browning, that evening of July 3, Lincoln talked to him further about the Sumter affair. He told Browning (as Browning recorded in his diary): "He himself conceived the idea, and proposed sending supplies, without attempting to reinforce, giving notice of the fact to Gov. Pickins [sic] of S.C. The plan succeeded. They attacked Sumter—it fell, and thus did more service than it otherwise could."[5]

7. Afterthoughts

1

TO MOST Northerners of the Civil War generation, it seemed obvious that the Southerners had started the war. The Southerners had fired the first shot and, what was worse, had done so without real provocation. They had begun the bloodshed on being informed that the Federal government would attempt to carry food to a few dozen hungry and beleaguered men.

To certain Northerners, however, and to practically all Southerners, it seemed just as obvious that Lincoln was to blame. While the war was still going on, one New York Democrat confided to another his suspicion that Lincoln had brought off an "adroit manoeuver" to "precipitate the attack" for its "expected effect upon the public feeling of the North." A one-time Kentucky governor, speaking in Liverpool, England, stated that the Republicans had schemed to "provoke a collision in order that they might say that the Confederates had made the first attack." The Richmond journalist E. A. Pollard wrote in his wartime history of the war that Lincoln had "procured" the assault and thus, by an "ingenious artifice," had himself commenced the fighting. "He chose to draw the sword," the *Petersburg Express* asserted, "but by a dirty trick succeeded in throwing upon the South the *seeming* blame of firing the first gun."

When, soon after the war's end, Alexander H. Stephens wrote his memoirs, he had no doubt as to who the real aggressor had been in 1861. In the book he conducted an imaginary colloquium. "Do you mean to say, Mr. Stephens, that the war was inaugurated by Mr. Lincoln?" he had one of his listeners ask. "Most assuredly I do," Stephens replied. "Why, how in the world . . . ?" the incredulous one persisted. "It is a fact that the *first gun* was fired by the Confederates," Stephens conceded. Then he patiently explained that the aggressor in a war is not the first to use force but the first to make force necessary.

Jefferson Davis, in his account of *The Rise and Fall of the Confederate Government* (1881), agreed with Stephens on this point, though he had agreed with him on little else while the two were president and vice president of the Confederacy. "He who makes the assault is not necessarily he who strikes the first blow or fires the first gun," Davis wrote. Referring to the Republicans and the Sumter expedition, he elaborated: "To have awaited further strengthening of their position by land and naval forces, with hostile purpose now declared, would have been as unwise as it would be to hesitate to strike down the arm of the assailant, who levels a deadly weapon at one's breast, until he has actually fired."[1]

Some Northerners, defenders of Lincoln, took a view rather similar to that of his Southern critics but presented it in a very different light. They praised Lincoln for essentially the same reasons that Davis, Stephens, and others blamed him.

In a book (1882) purporting to give the "true stories" of Sumter and Pickens, and dedicated to the "old friends" of Robert Anderson, a lieutenant colonel of the United States Army maintained that the advice of Scott and Seward to withdraw from Sumter was quite sound from a merely military standpoint. "But Mr. Lincoln and Mr. Blair judged more wisely that it would be better to sacrifice the garrison of Sumter for political effect." They sent the expedition "with the knowledge that it would compel the rebels to strike the first blow. If the last man in the garrison of Sumter had perished, it would have been a cheap price to pay for the magnificent outburst of patriotism that followed."

In their ten-volume history (1890) Lincoln's former private secretaries, John G. Nicolay and John Hay, wrote that Lincoln cared little whether the Sumter expedition would succeed in its provisioning attempt. "He was not playing a game of military strategy with Beauregard." He was playing a game for much higher stakes than Sumter itself. "When he finally gave the order that the fleet should sail he was master of the situation . . . master if the rebels hesitated or repented, because they would thereby forfeit their prestige with the South; master if they persisted, for he would then command a united North." He was "looking through and beyond the Sumter expedition to the now inevitable rebel attack and the response of an awakened and united North." The government, of course, was in the right. "But to make the issue sure, he determined in addition that the rebellion should be put in the wrong." His success entitled him to the high honors of "universal statesmanship."

In later generations a number of writers repeated the view that Lincoln himself had compelled the Confederates to fire first. Most of these writers inclined to the opinion that, in doing so, he exhibited less of universal statesmanship than of low cunning. Not till 1935, however, did a professional historian present a forthright statement of the thesis with all the accouterments of scholarship. In that year Professor Charles W. Ramsdell, of the University of Texas, reading a paper at the annual meeting of the American Historical Association, thus summed up the case:

"Lincoln, having decided that there was no other way than war for the salvation of his administration, his party, and the Union, maneuvered the Confederates into firing the first shot in order that they, rather than he, should take the blame of beginning bloodshed."

According to the Ramsdell argument, Davis and the rest of the Confederate leaders desired peace. They were eager to negotiate a settlement and avoid a resort to arms. But Lincoln, not so peaceably inclined, refused to deal with them.

During the weeks that followed his inauguration he was beset on two sides. Coercionists demanded that he take forceful action to rescue Fort Sumter. Moderate men advised him to yield the fort. If he should use force, he might impel the states of the Upper South to secede, and perhaps the border states as well. If he should abandon the fort, the majority of his party would probably abandon him. While he hesitated, his fellow Republicans bickered among themselves, his administration declined in prestige, and the country drifted toward ruin. He had to make up his mind soon, before the Sumter garrison was starved out.

At last he hit upon a way out of his dilemma. The thought occurred to him—*must have* occurred to him —that he could induce the Confederates to attack the fort. Then, the flag having been fired upon, he would gain all the benefits of an aroused patriotism. Republicans and Democrats would forget their quarrels of party and faction, the border states would respond with an upsurge of loyalty, and wavering millions throughout the North would rally to the Union cause. The party, the administration, and the Union would be saved.

The stratagem was a shrewd one, worthy of the shrewd man that Lincoln was. He decided to send the expedition and—most cleverly—to give advance notice. A genius with words, he could make them mean different things to different people. This is what he did with the words he addressed to the governor of South Carolina. To Northerners these words would seem quite innocent. The government was taking groceries to starving men and would not use force unless it had to. That was all. To Southerners the same words carried a threat, indeed a double threat. First, Sumter was going to be provisioned so that it could hold out. Second, if resistance should be offered, arms and men as well as food were going to be run in!

The notice was timed as carefully as it was phrased. It was delivered while the ships of the expedition were departing from New York. These could not reach their destination for three days at least, and so the Confederates would have plenty of time to take counteraction before the ships arrived. Already the Confederates had news that a sizable expedition was being prepared, and they were left to suppose that the entire force (including the part of it actually being dispatched to Pensacola) was heading for Charleston. With such a large force presumed to be on the way, they had all the more reason to move quickly.

The ruse worked perfectly. True, the expedition neither provisioned nor reinforced Sumter; it gave the garrison no help at all. But that was not the object. The object was to provoke a shot that would rouse the Northern people to fight.

This Ramsdell thesis was elaborated, with variations, in a book written by a Southern lawyer, John S. Tilley, and published during that fateful year 1941 (when another President was to be accused of a first-shot "maneuver"). Writing in a spirit more appropriate to a criminal court than a scholarly forum, Tilley contended that, at the time of Lincoln's inauguration, there existed no real need for provisioning Sumter. Indeed, Tilley left the impression that Lincoln had invented the story of short supplies at the fort so as to have an excuse for forcing the issue with the Confederacy. One of Tilley's chapter titles announced: "Lincoln Got What He

Wanted." The implication was that Lincoln wanted war and went out of his way to get it.[2]

While the Ramsdell thesis has attracted other and more responsible adherents, it has also been challenged by formidable critics. Professor James G. Randall, of the University of Illinois, maintained in the *Abraham Lincoln Quarterly* (1940) and in two books on Lincoln (1945, 1947) that Lincoln intended and expected a peaceful provisioning of the fort. After an independent study of *Lincoln and His Party in the Secession Crisis* (1942), Professor David M. Potter, then of Yale University (now of Stanford University), presented essentially similar conclusions. Lincoln counted upon a resurgence of Unionism in the South to overcome secession eventually, without war. To facilitate reunion, he planned to refrain from forcible assertion of Federal authority so long as he could do so without an obvious and outright surrender of it. He would have evacuated Fort Sumter if he had been able promptly enough to reinforce and secure Fort Pickens, so that it could serve as a substitute symbol of Federal authority. Events, however, compelled him to act. Finally he accepted the necessity of the Sumter expedition, but he took care to make it as unprovocative as possible. By means of it he hoped merely to preserve the existing status in Charleston Harbor. His policy was a failure, since it culminated in war. Such is the contention of Professors Randall and Potter.

In between the Randall-Potter thesis of the peace policy and the Ramsdell-Tilley thesis of the war maneuver, there is yet a third interpretation which sees

Lincoln's policy as aiming at neither war nor peace, as such, but as risking the chance of war. Professor Kenneth M. Stampp, of the University of California, stated this thesis of the calculated risk in the *Journal of Southern History* (1945) and restated it in his book *And the War Came* (1950). According to Stampp, Lincoln's primary purpose was to preserve the Union and to do so by a "strategy of defense" which would avoid even the appearance of initiating hostilities.[3]

2

ONE VERSION of the Sumter story—Tilley's insinuation that Lincoln faked the hunger crisis at the fort—may be immediately ruled out. This insinuation was based mainly upon the absence of evidence. Tilley could not find the letter, or even a copy of the letter, that Lincoln was supposed to have seen on the day after his inauguration, the letter in which Major Anderson revealed shortages of certain essential supplies and the necessity of either replenishing these or abandoning the fort. Now, it may be good legal practice to argue from the absence of evidence. It is not sound historical scholarship. Even at the time Tilley wrote, there were documents available referring to the Anderson letter and indicating clearly enough that it actually had been written and sent. Later, after the opening of the Robert Todd Lincoln Collection of Lincoln papers in the Library of Congress, in 1947, lo!

there was the missing letter which Tilley had been at such pains to prove nonexistent.[4]

The Ramsdell thesis itself does not necessarily fall with the collapse of Tilley's case, though much of Ramsdell's evidence is either inconclusive or irrelevant. He devoted a considerable part of his essay merely to showing that various pressures or supposed pressures had induced Lincoln to decide in favor of sending the Sumter expedition, but this line of argument has little bearing upon the main issue to which Ramsdell had addressed himself. As his critic Randall aptly commented: "The inducing-to-attack argument does not proceed very far before it involves a subtle change of approach, so that the very decision to send the expedition is treated as the aggressive or provocative thing, whereas the point at issue . . . is whether the sending of supplies to feed the garrison was not in Lincoln's mind compatible with continued peace efforts."[5]

This is indeed a crucial question. It may be restated thus: Did Lincoln think, or did he have good reason to think, that he could send his expedition to Sumter and his advance notice to the South Carolina governor without encountering resistance on the part of the Confederate forces at Charleston? Unfortunately, there is no direct, contemporary evidence to show what Lincoln *actually thought* about the probable Confederate reaction. There is, however, plenty of evidence to indicate what he *had good reason to think.*

Lincoln was familiar with the news of recent events at Charleston—events illustrating the readiness of the Confederate batteries to open up. He knew that in

January his predecessor, President Buchanan, had sent an unescorted and unarmed merchant steamer with provisions and (below deck) troops for Sumter, and that the Charleston batteries had fired upon this vessel and compelled her to turn back. Now, Lincoln was sending not one ship but several, including warships. He had reason to expect that his expedition would meet with at least the same degree of hostility as Buchanan's had met with, if not more. Before Lincoln's expedition had actually sailed, he received confirmation of this probability in the report that, on April 3, the Confederate batteries fired upon the Boston schooner *R. H. Shannon*, which innocently had put in at Charleston Harbor to get out of the ocean fog.

When Lincoln called upon his cabinet for written advice, on March 15 and again on March 29, he got little assurance the first time and still less the second time that a peaceful provisioning would be likely. The first time only two of the seven members favored making the attempt, and only one of the two, Secretary Chase, was confident that it could be made without armed conflict. The second time only one definitely opposed the attempt, but even Chase, who still favored it, had lost his confidence that it could be carried out peaceably. Secretary Welles, who had changed from opposition to approval, now expressed an opinion similar to Chase's. "There is little possibility that this will be permitted," Welles stated, "if the opposing forces can prevent it."

The objection may be raised that, nevertheless, Lincoln had reason to think *his* Sumter expedition, unlike

Buchanan's, might be tolerated by the authorities in Charleston because he intended to give, and did give, advance notice of its coming, whereas Buchanan had not done so. Though Ramsdell has characterized this notice as a threat, and a double-barreled one at that, his critics have replied that it was no such thing. They say it was given "to show that hostile surprise was not intended" and to make clear Lincoln's "non-aggressive purpose." Whether the notification, with its reference to "men, arms, or ammunition," constituted a threat, we need not stop to debate. We need only to recall what Lincoln had learned recently from Hurlbut, his secret emissary to Charleston. Hurlbut reported his conclusion "that a ship known to contain *only provisions* for Sumpter would be stopped & refused admittance." In the light of this information, Lincoln would have had little ground for expecting that his notice would mollify the Confederates even if he had confined it to a simple announcement that he would attempt to supply "provisions only."

If Lincoln had intended and expected nothing but a peaceful provisioning, he no doubt would have been surprised and disappointed at the actual outcome. In fact, however, he repeatedly expressed a feeling of at least qualified satisfaction and success. When he replied to the Virginia delegates at the White House, on April 13, he said in an almost triumphant tone that the "unprovoked assault" would set him "at liberty" to go beyond the self-imposed limitations of his inaugural and to "repossess" as well as "hold, occupy, and possess" Federal positions in the seceded states. When he consoled the frustrated Fox, on May 1, he wrote: "You and I both anticipated that the cause of the country would be advanced by making the attempt to provision Fort-Sumpter, even if it should fail; and it is no small consolation now to feel that our anticipation is justified by the result." When he drafted his first message to Congress, for the July 4 session, he emphasized the point that, by the "affair at Fort Sumpter," he had succeeded in making good his earlier declaration that, if war should come, the seceders would have to be the aggressors. And when he read the message to Browning, on July 3, he went on to remark, as Browning paraphrased him: "The plan succeeded. They attacked Sumter—it fell, and thus, did more service than it otherwise could."

In short, it appears that Lincoln, when he decided to send the Sumter expedition, considered hostilities to be *probable*. It also appears, however, that he believed an unopposed and peaceable provisioning to be at least barely *possible*. It is reasonable to suppose that he shared the expectation of his Attorney General, who wrote in his diary at the time Fox was leaving New York for Charleston: "One of two things will happen —either the fort will be well provisioned, the Southrons forebearing to assail the boats, or a fierce contest will ensue." If the first rather than the second of the two possibilities had materialized, then Lincoln doubtless could have said afterwards, just as he said when the second of the two occurred, that his plan had succeeded. Doubtless he would have been equally well satisfied, perhaps even better satisfied. Either way, whether the

Confederates resisted or not, he would have been (in the words of Nicolay and Hay) "master of the situation."

It follows, then, that neither the Randall-Potter nor the Ramsdell view of Lincoln's intentions and expectations seems quite accurate. On the one hand, Lincoln did not count confidently upon peace, though he thought there was a bare chance of its being preserved for the time being. On the other hand, he did not deliberately provoke war. He thought hostilities would be the likely result, and he was determined that, if they should be, they must clearly be initiated by the Confederates. "To say that Lincoln meant that the first shot would be fired by the other side *if a first shot was fired*," as Randall has most admirably put the matter, "is not to say that he maneuvered to have the first shot fired."[6]

3

THE Ramsdell thesis, with its war-maneuver charge, is essentially an effort to document the rationalizations of Davis, Stephens, and other Confederates or Confederate sympathizers. Similarly, the Randall-Potter thesis, in one of its important aspects, is essentially an effort to substantiate the explanation that Lincoln gave after the events, in his July 4 message to Congress.

Interestingly, Potter observes that, to understand Lincoln's plans at the time of his inauguration, "it is necessary to exclude the misleading perspective of hindsight, and to view the problem as he viewed it at the time, rather than as he later viewed it." Yet, in dealing with Lincoln's policy after the inauguration, Potter neglects this very principle. Like Randall, he bases his argument largely on the misleading perspective of hindsight, on the way Lincoln viewed the problem in July rather than the way he viewed it in March and April.

According to Potter, who paraphrases Lincoln's July 4 message, the Sumter expedition was only tentative, the Pickens expedition definite. The Sumter expedition "was withheld until the fort was almost starved out, and it was withheld because Lincoln still hoped that he could transfer the issue of Union to Fort Pickens before the Sumter question reached a crisis." To both Potter and Randall the critical date is April 6. This was the date when, as Lincoln said in the message, he received a report that his order to land the troops already on shipboard in Pensacola Harbor, to reinforce Fort Pickens, had not been carried out. And this was the date when Lincoln sent to Major Anderson, by special messenger, the letter informing him that the expedition was going ahead (though the letter was dated April 4). "Up to April 6, then," Randall says, "the expedition, though prepared, could have been held back." And the plain implication of Randall and Potter, as well as of Lincoln himself, is that if the troops had been landed at Fort Pickens, and if Lincoln had known of it by April 6, he would have called off the Sumter expedition.[7]

There is undoubtedly an element of truth in this

story of a Sumter-for-Pickens sacrifice. During March and early April the idea was discussed in the newspapers, was recommended by a number of Lincoln's Republican correspondents, and was urged again and again by Seward. At one time or another, Lincoln must have given some consideration to it. He could hardly have avoided doing so. Possibly, if he had been assured before March 29 that the troops had been landed and Fort Pickens was safe, he might not have decided at that time to prepare the Sumter expedition. But it appears (in the light of contemporary evidence) that, having ordered the Sumter preparations on March 29, he did not thereafter make his policy for Charleston contingent upon events at Pensacola.

Actually, the key dates regarding the Sumter decision are March 29 and April 4, not April 6. After the order for preparations had been given on March 29, there followed a period of vacillation and delay which was exasperating to Fox. The causes were twofold: the fears that visible preparations would hurt the prospects on the New York money market for the government loan to be subscribed on April 2, and the hopes (on the part of Seward) that a last-minute Sumter-for-Virginia deal could be arranged. After the successful sale of the bonds, and after the fiasco of Lincoln's conversation with the Virginia representative, Lincoln decided definitely to go ahead with the Sumter plans. On April 4 he arranged the details with Fox and wrote the letter informing Anderson that supplies would be on the way. That same day a copy of the letter was mailed to Anderson, and Anderson received it three days later. Not sure that the mail had got through Lincoln sent the second copy by special messenger on April 6. His sending it on that day is no indication whatever that he waited until then to make his final decision regarding Sumter.[8]

True, on April 6, Lincoln learned that his nearly-a-month-old order to land the troops at Pensacola had not been executed. But, to him, this was hardly unexpected news: it was merely a confirmation of what he already had guessed. As early as March 29 he had suspected that the order somehow had gone astray. On April 1 he was informed, by a communication from Pensacola, that the forces there had (as of March 21) been out of touch with the government. When the report of April 6 arrived, it had only one visible effect upon the administration: it caused the prompt dispatch of a messenger overland to Pensacola with new orders from Secretary Welles to land the troops already there.

Meanwhile, Seward had never given up his obsession with the idea of yielding Sumter and holding Pickens as a kind of substitute. The idea was Seward's, not Lincoln's. Seward stressed it in his brash April 1 memorandum, "Some Thoughts for the President's Consideration," and Lincoln in his written reply on the same day said his own domestic policy was the same as Seward's "with the single exception, that it does not propose to abandon Fort Sumter."

Why, then, did Lincoln tell Congress, in the July 4 message, that he *had* proposed to abandon Fort Sumter if Fort Pickens could be made secure in time? One conceivable reason is that, after the months of preoc-

cupation with the widening war, he had forgotten some
of the chronological details of his earlier policy forma-
tion. He may well have remembered that on some occasion or other, possibly in mid-March, he had actually
given at least fleeting consideration to the proposal. He
may not have remembered exactly when, or how seri-
ously. Another conceivable reason is that he was still
concerned, in July, about the opinions of those peace-
minded Northerners, including many Republicans,
who in March and early April had been willing or even
eager for Sumter to be evacuated on the condition that
Pickens be firmly held. Lincoln may have felt it advisable now to reassure those timid and hesitant ones that
he had, indeed, exhausted all the possibilities for peace
and, in particular, had carefully considered the Sumter-
for-Pickens alternative.

In stressing this alternative as an essential element of
Lincoln's April policy, Randall and Potter confuse
Lincoln's March and April thinking with Seward's.
They make the same error in characterizing Lincoln's
overall approach to the secession problem. Potter, for
instance, asserts that "Republican policy was consistent" and that party leaders "insisted that delay and
avoidance of friction would create a condition under
which the Unionists in the South could regain the as-
cendancy."[9] Certain party leaders, yes, and above all
Seward, but Lincoln never fully shared Seward's faith
in the do-nothing panacea.

In truth, Republican policy was far from being consistent. The policy of Seward was, at many points, inconsistent with that of Lincoln. The assumption that

time would heal all wounds, the hints and promises of an early withdrawal from Sumter, the notion of bargaining Sumter for Virginia, the proposal to abandon Sumter and concentrate on Pickens—all these were hobbies of Seward's. Lincoln had great respect for Seward's abilities and for his political value to the administration. He listened to Seward's suggestions and urgings. To some extent he was influenced by them, but he was by no means converted. Nor did he authorize all of Seward's undertakings. Some of them he knew nothing about until after they had been well advanced.

4

THE worst fault in the Ramsdell thesis is a lack of balance and perspective. Ramsdell makes Lincoln appear too much the warmonger, Davis too much the peace lover; Lincoln too much the controlling force, Davis too much the passive agent. Ramsdell argues that the Confederate government "could not, without yielding the principle of independence, abate its claims to the fort." He fails to see that, likewise, the Federal government could not abate its claims without yielding the principle of Union.

Davis made the decision that led directly to war. True, early on the morning of April 12, Beauregard sent Roger A. Pryor, James Chestnut, and two others from Charleston to the fort to present Davis's final terms, and these men on their own rejected Anderson's reply—which was that he would hold his fire and evacuate in three days, unless he should meanwhile receive "controlling instructions" or "additional supplies." Instead of taking responsibility upon themselves, Pryor and the other hot-headed underlings might have referred Anderson's reply to Beauregard, and he in turn to Walker and Davis. Since Pryor and his colleagues went ahead without thus referring to higher authority, the story arose that they and not Davis had made the real decision. The story seemed to be confirmed by the testimony that Pryor gave to an historian many years later, in 1909. Accepting Pryor's account, the historian wrote: "Pryor and his associates did not report to the General, but, thinking that Davis was trying to reconstruct the Union and negotiate with Seward to that end and that the chance of war was about to slip away forever, they conferred together and decided to give the signal to the gunners to fire—and war began, and such a war!"[10] War began, all right, but the main point of Pryor's testimony has no foundation in fact. When Pryor and his associates rejected Anderson's reply, they were faithfully following the line of Davis's policy, and Davis afterwards fully approved what they had done. The real decision was his, not theirs.

Davis justified his decision on the ground that "the reduction of Fort Sumter was a measure of defense rendered absolutely and immediately necessary." In fact, however, Sumter in April, 1861, offered no immediate threat to the physical safety of Charleston or of South Carolina or of the other six Confederate states.

Nor did the approach of Fox's small fleet suddenly create such a threat. The landing of supplies—or even of men, arms, and ammunition—would have made little difference in the existing power balance.

Writers of the Ramsdell school insist that there was no *military* reason for Lincoln's effort to provision the fort. They cannot have it both ways. If there was no military reason for Lincoln's attempt, there could have been none for Davis' effort to forestall it.

Indeed, the Ramsdell thesis, turned inside out, could be applied to Davis with as much justice as it has been applied to Lincoln. One could argue that political and not military necessity led Davis to order the firing of the first shot. The very life of the Confederacy, the growth upon which that life depended, was at stake. So were the pride, the prestige, and the position of Davis. Ramsdell himself, a distinguished authority on Confederate history, might appropriately have devoted his talents to an essay on "Davis and Fort Sumter" instead of "Lincoln and Fort Sumter."

Biographers of Davis and historians of the Confederacy have evaded or obscured their hero's role in the Sumter affair. They have digressed to levy accusations or innuendoes at Lincoln. If they have any concern for historical objectivity, however, they should face frankly the question of Davis's responsibility for the coming of the war. Upon them, upon *his* partisans, should rest the burden of proof. It should not have to be borne forever, as it has for far too many years, by Lincoln's champions. After all, Lincoln did not order the guns to fire. Davis did.[11]

AUTHORITIES agree pretty well as to what actually happened in March and April, 1861. They disagree about the meaning of the events and, in particular, about the aims of Lincoln. To judge historical significance involves a certain amount of guessing, and to ascertain a man's intentions (especially when the man is so close-mouthed as Lincoln or, for that matter, Davis) requires a bit of mind reading. For these reasons, the true inwardness of the Sumter story will, in some of its aspects, always be more or less moot. The probable truth may be summarized as follows:

At the time of his inauguration Lincoln was determined to retake the Federal positions already lost to the seceding states as well as to hold the positions not yet lost. When he revised his inaugural, so as to announce only the "hold, occupy, and possess" objective, he did not really change or limit his original purpose. He meant to achieve this purpose, however, without appearing to initiate the use of force. He did not yet know precisely how he was going to manage so delicate a task, but he assumed that he would have plenty of time in which to deal with the problem.

Then, for about three weeks, he hesitated with regard to Fort Sumter, though not with regard to Fort Pickens, which he promptly ordered to be reinforced by means of the troops already available there. In the case of Sumter, the bad news from Anderson and the deterring counsel from Scott and the cabinet gave him pause. During the period of hesitation he considered alternative lines of action as at least temporary expedients—the collection of customs on ships off Southern ports, the evacuation of Sumter if and when Pickens had been made absolutely secure, the provisioning (with advance notice) but not the reinforcing of Sumter.

On March 29 he gave orders for the preparation of an expedition to provision Sumter—and also, conditionally, to reinforce it. He had decided to act because, from various sources of advice and information, he had concluded that a retreat at any point (except in the face of superior force) would lead eventually to a retreat at all points. If he were to yield to the demand for Sumter, he would still face the demand for Pickens and the other Florida forts, to say nothing of the demand for recognition of the Confederacy. True, if he took a stand, he would run the risk of antagonizing and losing Virginia and other still-loyal slave states. But if he declined to take a stand, he would still risk losing those states, through conferring new prestige and attractiveness upon the Confederacy. And, besides, he would surely alienate many of his adherents in the North.

Soon afterward, at Seward's urging, Lincoln ordered also the preparation of another expedition, this one to be secret, unannounced, and intended for the immediate reinforcement of Fort Pickens. Even its sponsor,

Seward, did not expect the enterprise to be peaceably received: he merely thought Pensacola a better place than Charleston for war to begin. The Pickens expedition got off first, the Sumter preparations running into various snags, including Seward's efforts at sabotage.

On April 4, in consultation with Fox, Lincoln made the final arrangements for the Sumter effort. According to these carefully laid plans, Fox's men would try to run in supplies by boats or tugs. If challenged, the pilot would hand over a note explaining that the aim was only to take food to the garrison, and that if the Confederates fired upon the boats, they would be firing upon unarmed and defenseless men. Already the South Carolina governor would have received his notice. Thus the arrival of the boats would put the Confederates in a dilemma. If they fired, they would convict themselves of an atrocity. If not, they could hardly prevent the fort from being supplied. Either way, they would lose.

And if they fired, the guns of the warships offshore and of the fort itself would fire back and, hopefully, clear the way for the supplies to be taken in, along with reinforcements. This would, no doubt, entail a certain amount of bloodshed, but surely the Federal government would appear to be justified, in the eyes of most Northerners and of many Southerners as well. Even the majority of Virginians, under these circumstances, would possibly think twice before countenancing the secession of their state.

In certain respects the outcome was not to be quite what Lincoln anticipated.

The policy of the Montgomery government was less passive, less cautious, than he supposed. That policy aimed to get control of Sumter and the other forts as soon as it could be done, by negotiations if feasible, by siege or assault if not. The mission to Washington had a twofold function: on the one hand, to seek recognition of the Confederacy and a peaceful transfer of the forts and, on the other, to gain time for military preparations to be used in case diplomacy should fail. Once the preparations had proceeded far enough, the termination of diplomacy was to be the signal for the beginning of military measures. By early April, in Charleston, Beauregard was ready. Soon he would have begun actual operations for taking Sumter—even if Lincoln had never planned or sent an expedition of any kind (unless Anderson should promptly have given up, which was a possibility, or Lincoln should have invited the commissioners to talk with him, which was not).

When Davis heard of Lincoln's notice to the South Carolina governor, on April 8, his immediate response was to order Beauregard to prevent the landing of the supplies. It is interesting to speculate about what might have happened if Davis had stuck to this decision. Most likely, Beauregard then would have waited for the actual approach of the provisioning boats. But Fox, considering the storm-caused delays and the nonappearance of the flagship, *Powhatan*, probably would have decided not to send the boats in. In that event, the Sumter expedition would have proved an utter fiasco. Lincoln would have lost prestige and Davis gained it. Or, after hesitation, Fox might have made a token effort. Then things would have happened pretty much as Lincoln had calculated, except that the expedition would not have had the power to open the way for the supplies.

But Davis and his advisers did not remain content with their decision of April 8. Two days later they made a new one, and orders went to Beauregard to demand a surrender and, failing to get that, to reduce the fort.

This reaction, though more than Lincoln had counted on, was somewhat better, from his point of view, than the previous one. If the Confederates were going to fire at all, it was well that they should do so without even waiting until the food-laden boats were in sight. The eagerness of the Confederates would the more surely convict them of aggression, and this was all to the good, even though it would mean that Sumter would have less chance of being actually reinforced and held.

The first shot having been fired, the response of the North more than reconciled Lincoln to the loss of the fort, if not also to the loss of Virginia, Arkansas, Tennessee, and North Carolina. The response of the North certainly went far toward making possible the ultimate redemption of the Union.

In those early April days both Lincoln and Davis took chances which, in retrospect, seem awesome. The chances they took eventuated in the most terrible of all wars for the American people. Lincoln and Davis, as each made his irrevocable decision, could see clearly enough the cost of holding back. Neither could see so clearly the cost of going ahead. Both expected, or at least hoped, that the hostilities would be limited in space and time. Lincoln thought of blockade and boycott and a few seaborne operations against coastal forts. Davis thought of accessions and allies—in the slave states, in foreign countries, and in the North itself— which would make the Confederacy too strong for its independence to be long contested.

The Sumter incident itself did not lead at once to general war. Neither side was yet prepared for that. By a kind of escalation, however, war rapidly developed, and the lines were soon drawn. Through his proclamation of April 15, calling for 75,000 volunteers, Lincoln unintentionally contributed to the growth of the martial spirit on both sides. Perhaps if in that proclamation he had stressed his defensive purposes, especially the need for troops to protect the capital, he might at least have strengthened the Unionists in Virginia and the other non-seceded slave states.

The charge of "aggression," which has been bandied for so long, should not concern historians except as it figured in the propaganda of 1861 and after. From the Confederate point of view the United States had made itself the aggressor long before Lincoln acted to strengthen any fort. It was aggression when, on December 26, 1860, Major Anderson moved his small force from their exposed position at Fort Moultrie to the somewhat more secure one at Fort Sumter. Indeed, it was a continuing act of aggression every day that United States forces remained in Sumter or any other place within the boundaries of the Confederacy. And from the Union point of view the Confederacy had committed and was committing aggression by its very claim to existence, to say nothing of its seizures of Federal property and its preparations to seize Sumter and Pickens. Viewed impartially, both sides were guilty of aggression, and neither was.

When Lincoln expressed his desire for peace he was sincere, and so was Davis when he did the same. But Lincoln thought of peace for one, undivided country; Davis, of peace for two separate countries. "Both parties deprecated war," as Lincoln later put it, "but one of them would *make* war rather than let the nation survive; and the other would *accept* war rather than let it perish. And the war came."[12]

BIBLIOGRAPHY

Primary Sources

This book (except for the concluding chapter) is based directly and almost entirely upon the words of Lincoln and his contemporaries. Especially important is the correspondence of Lincoln. Incoming mail, along with cabinet memoranda and other miscellany, is preserved in the Robert Todd Lincoln Collection of manuscripts in the Library of Congress. Lincoln's letters and speeches are readily available in *The Collected Works of Abraham Lincoln,* excellently edited by Roy P. Basler and others (9 vols., 1953–55). Political as well as military and naval documents are contained in the government-published series entitled *War of the Rebellion: . . . Official Records of the Union and Confederate Armies* (128 vols., 1880–1901) and *Official Records of the Union and Confederate Navies in the War of the Rebellion* (26 vols., 1894–1922). Other writings by contemporaries include the following:

Baldwin, J. B. *Interview between President Lincoln and John B. Baldwin, April 4, 1861* (1866).

Bates, Edward. *The Diary of Edward Bates, 1859–1866,* edited by H. K. Beale (1933).

Botts, J. M. *The Great Rebellion* (1866).

Browning, O. H. *The Diary of Orville Hickman Browning,* edited by T. C. Pease and J. G. Randall (2 vols., 1925–33).

Campbell, J. A. "Papers of John A. Campbell, 1861–1865," in *Southern Historical Society Papers*, n.s., IV (1917), 3–81.

Davis, Jefferson. *The Rise and Fall of the Confederate Government* (2 vols., 1881).

De Leon, T. C. *Four Years in Rebel Capitals* (1890).

Doubleday, Abner. *Reminiscences of Forts Sumter and Moultrie in 1860–'61* (1876).

Dumond, D. L., ed. *Southern Editorials on Secession* (1931).

Fox, G. V. *Confidential Correspondence of Gustavus Vasa Fox*, edited by R. M. Thompson and R. Wainwright (2 vols., 1918).

Gobright, L. A. *Recollections of Men and Things at Washington* (1869).

Lamon, W. H. *Recollections of Abraham Lincoln* (1911)

Magruder, A. B. "A Piece of Secret History: President Lincoln and the Virginia Convention of 1861," in the *Atlantic Monthly*, XXXV (1875), 438–45.

Meigs, M. C. "Diary, March 29–April 8, 1861," in the *American Historical Review*, XXVI (1920–21), 285–303.

Perkins, H. C., ed. *Northern Editorials on Secession* (2 vols., 1942).

Porter, D. D. *Incidents and Anecdotes of the Civil War* (1885).

Russell, W. H. *My Diary North and South* (1863). New edition, condensed, by Fletcher Pratt (1954).

Schurz, Carl. *The Reminiscences of Carl Schurz* (3 vols., 1917).

Stephens, A. H. *A Constitutional View of the Late War between the States* (2 vols., 1868–70).

Strong, G. T. *The Diary of George Templeton Strong*, edited by Allan Nevins and M. H. Thomas (4 vols., 1952).

Welles, Gideon. *Diary of Gideon Welles*, edited by J. T.

BIBLIOGRAPHY

Morse, Jr. (3 vols., 1911). Corrected edition by H. K. Beale and A. W. Brownsword (3 vols., 1960).

Welling, J. C. "The Proposed Evacuation of Fort Sumter," in the *Nation*, XXIX (December 4, 1879), 383–84.

Secondary Sources

Many of the following provide useful information and insights, and some contain quotations of primary materials not easily to be found elsewhere. Others are relevant only as illustrations of the range of possible viewpoints with regard to Lincoln and Fort Sumter. The listing is selective and by no means complete.

Anderson, T. M. *The Political Conspiracies Preceding the Rebellion, or The True Stories of Sumter and Pickens* (1882).

Bancroft, Frederic. *The Life of William H. Seward* (2 vols., 1900).

Colton, R. C. *The Civil War in the Western Territories* (1959).

Crawford, S. W. *The Genesis of the Civil War: The Story of Sumter, 1860–61* (1887).

Geyl, Peter. "The American Civil War and the Problem of Inevitability," in the *New England Quarterly*, XXIV (1951), 147–68.

Greeley, Horace. *The American Conflict: A History of the Great Rebellion* (2 vols., 1864).

Gunderson, R. G. "William C. Rives and the 'Old Gentlemen's Convention,'" in the *Journal of Southern History*, XXII (1956), 459–76.

Hall, W. L. "Lincoln's Interview with John B. Baldwin," in the *South Atlantic Quarterly*, XIII (1914), 260–69.

Hesseltine, W. B. *Lincoln and the War Governors* (1948).

Lutz, R. H. "Rudolf Schleiden and the Visit to Richmond,

April 25, 1861," in the *Annual Report of the American Historical Association for the Year 1915* (1917), pp. 209–16.

Nevins, Allan. *The War for the Union:* Volume I, *The Improvised War, 1861–1862* (1959).

Nicolay, J. G. *The Outbreak of the Rebellion* (1881).

—— and John Hay. *Abraham Lincoln: A History* (10 vols., 1890).

Potter, D. M. *Lincoln and His Party in the Secession Crisis* (1942). Softcover edition, with new preface (1962).

Pressly, T. J. *Americans Interpret Their Civil War* (1954).

Ramsdell, C. W. "Lincoln and Fort Sumter," in the *Journal of Southern History*, III (1937), 259–88.

Randall, J. G. *Lincoln the Liberal Statesman* (1947).

——. *Lincoln the President: Springfield to Gettysburg* (2 vols., 1945).

Shanks, H. T. *The Secession Movement in Virginia, 1847–1861* (1934).

Smith, W. E. *The Francis Preston Blair Family in Politics* (2 vols., 1933).

Stampp, K. M. *And the War Came: The North and the Secession Crisis, 1860–1861* (1950).

——. "Lincoln and the Strategy of Defense in the Crisis of 1861," in the *Journal of Southern History*, XI (1945), 297–323.

Swanberg, W. A. *First Blood: The Story of Fort Sumter* (1958).

Tilley, J. S. *Lincoln Takes Command* (1941).

Tomes, Robert. *The War with the South* (1862).

White, L. A. *Robert Barnwell Rhett: Father of Secession* (1931).

NOTES

Foreword

1. Quoted by Louis Morton, "From Fort Sumter to Poland: The Question of War Guilt," in *World Politics*, XIV (1962), 389.

2. In the spring of 1962, President Kennedy was quoted as saying that the United States must be prepared to take the initiative, under certain circumstances, in using nuclear weapons. The Russian newspaper *Pravda* then accused Kennedy of preaching the doctrine of a preventive nuclear attack. A State Department spokesman explained, however, that the United States should strike a first atomic blow "only in retaliation for a massive conventional assault, say a big push by the Red army that threatened to engulf Western Europe." See the *Wisconsin State Journal* (Madison), March 28, 1962, sec. 1, p. 9, cols. 3–6; the *New York Times*, April 1, 1962, sec. 1, p. 1, col. 6; and the *San Francisco Examiner*, April 15, 1962, sec. 1, p. 1, col. 7.

3. R. N. Current, *The Lincoln Nobody Knows* (1958), pp. 104–5.

4. For an introduction to the Pearl Harbor controversy, see R. N. Current, "How Stimson Meant to 'Maneuver' the Japanese," in the *Mississippi Valley Historical Review*, XL (1953), 67–74.

Chapter 1

1. All these quotations are from Roy P. Basler and others, eds., *The Collected Works of Abraham Lincoln* (9 vols., 1953–55), IV, 159, 194–96, 236–37, 241–45, 254, 256.

2. On Seward, see Robert Tomes, *The War with the South* (1862), pp. 41–43, 103, 124; Allan Nevins, *The Improvised War, 1861–1862* (1959), pp. 37–38; R. H. Lutz, "Rudolph Schleiden and the Visit to Richmond, April 25, 1861," in the *Annual Report of the American Historical Association for the Year 1915* (1917), p. 210.

3. Blair to G. V. Fox, January 31, 1861, in *Confidential Correspondence of Gustavus Vasa Fox*, ed. by R. M. Thompson and R. Wainwright (2 vols., 1918), I, 4–5.

4. On the Virginia situation, see H. T. Shanks, *The Secession Movement in Virginia, 1847–1861* (1934), pp. 140, 155, 176; J. F. Rhodes, *History of the United States from . . . 1850 to [1877]* (7 vols., 1893–1900), III, 300; D. L. Dumond, ed., *Southern Editorials on Secession*, p. 345; S. Clemens to Lincoln, March 4, 1861, in the Robert Todd Lincoln Collection.

5. Shanks, *Secession Movement*, pp. 168–69, 175; Lutz, in *Annual Report of the A.H.A. for 1915*, pp. 210–11; Nevins, *Improvised War*, pp. 46–47; R. G. Gunderson, "William C. Rives and the 'Old Gentlemen's Convention,'" in the *Journal of Southern History*, XXII (1956), 471–72.

6. J. G. Nicolay and John Hay, *Abraham Lincoln: A History* (10 vols., 1890), III, 369–71.

7. *Collected Works*, IV, 254, 261; Nicolay and Hay, *Lincoln*, III, 321, 336.

8. For human-interest details regarding the Washington scene, Lincoln's arrival and daily routine, the inaugural procession, and the inauguration, see Tomes, *War with the South*, p. 112; Nicolay and Hay, *Lincoln*, III, 326, 344; L.

NOTES

A. Gobright, *Recollections of Men and Things at Washington* (1869), pp. 287–90; W. H. Russell, *My Diary North and South,* ed. by Fletcher Pratt (1954), pp. 17–18, 195; T. C. De Leon, *Four Years in Rebel Capitals* (1890), pp. 19–20; J. G. Randall, *Lincoln the President: Springfield to Gettysburg* (2 vols., 1945), I, 294; Margaret Leech, *Reveille in Washington, 1860–1865* (1941), pp. 35–45.

Chapter 2

1. Ruth Painter Randall, *Mary Lincoln: Biography of a Marriage* (1953), p. 212.

2. Joseph Holt and Winfield Scott to Lincoln, March 5, 1861, in the R. T. L. Collection; Holt and Isaac Toucey to James Glynn and others, January 29, 1861, in *War of the Rebellion:* . . . *Official Records of the Union and Confederate Armies* (128 vols., 1880–1901), ser. I, vol. I, pp. 355–56; Nicolay and Hay, *Lincoln,* III, 376–77, 379; J. G. Nicolay, *The Outbreak of the Rebellion* (1881), p. 38.

3. Leech, *Reveille,* p. 40; Russell, *Diary* (Pratt ed.), pp. 26–28; *The Diary of Edward Bates, 1859–1866,* ed. by H. K. Beale (1933), p. 177; *The Diary of Gideon Welles,* ed. by J. T. Morse, Jr. (3 vols., 1911), I, 3–6, 29; *Official Records,* ser. I, vol. I, pp. 197, 360; Holt to Lincoln, March 9, 1861, Nicolay to Scott, March 9, 1861, Scott to Lincoln, March 11, 1861, Scott to Anderson, March 11, 1861, all in the R. T. L. Collection.

4. Dumond, *Southern Editorials,* p. 474; Shanks, *Secession Movement,* pp. 181–82; F. Bancroft, *The Life of William H. Seward* (2 vols., 1900), II, 103–15; *Official Records,* ser. I, vol. I, p. 196; Nevins, *Improvised War,* pp. 41–43; *The Diary of George Templeton Strong,* ed. by Allan Nevins and M. H. Thomas (4 vols., 1952), I, 108–10; J. C. Welling,

in the *Nation*, XXIX (December 4, 1879), 383–84; Seward to Lincoln, March 9, Hicks to Lincoln, March 11, W. C. Wickham to Scott, March 11, 1861, all in the R. T. L. Collection.

5. *Collected Works*, IV, 284–85; N. P. Tallmadge to Seward, March 7, Webb to Lincoln, March 12, F. P. Blair to Montgomery Blair, March 12, Scott to Lincoln, March 12, 1861, and Abner Doubleday to Mrs. Doubleday (n.d.), all in the R. T. L. Collection; Fox, *Confidential Correspondence*, I, 8–9; Bates, *Diary*, pp. 177–78; Tomes, *War with the South*, pp. 140–41; Nevins, *Improvised War*, pp. 42–45; Abner Doubleday, *Reminiscences of Forts Sumter and Moultrie in 1860–'61* (1876), pp. 130, 150; W. A. Swanberg, *First Blood: The Story of Fort Sumter* (1958), pp. 168, 235–36, 238.

6. Gilmer to Seward, March 9, Wickham to Scott, March 11, T. P. Shaffner to Lincoln, March 11, cabinet members to Lincoln, March 15 and 16, Lincoln to Chase and Bates, March 18, and Welles to Lincoln, March 20, 1861, all in the R. T. L. Collection; *Collected Works*, IV, 288–90; *Official Records*, ser. I, vol. I, pp. 196–98; Strong, *Diary*, p. 111; Nevins, *Improvised War*, pp. 46–48; W. E. Smith, *The Francis Preston Blair Family in Politics* (2 vols., 1933), II, 9–10.

Chapter 3

1. Hurlbut to Lincoln, March 27, 1861, in the R. T. L. Collection; *Official Records*, ser. I, vol. I, pp. 221–22, 282; Fox, *Confidential Correspondence*, I, 9–11; Doubleday, *Reminiscences*, p. 134; Russell, *Diary* (Pratt ed.), pp. 19–27, 73; Nicolay and Hay, *Lincoln*, III, 389–92; Bancroft, *Seward*, II, 107; Nevins, *Improvised War*, pp. 48–49.

2. Abner Doubleday to Mrs. Doubleday, March 29, and

cabinet memoranda, March 29 and 30, 1861, in the R. T. L. Collection; *Collected Works*, IV, 301; Bates, *Diary*, p. 180; Strong, *Diary*, p. 112; Nicolay and Hay, *Lincoln*, III, 394–95; Bancroft, *Seward*, II, 123, 126–28; Russell, *Diary* (Pratt ed.), pp. 28–29; Nevins, *Improvised War*, pp. 54–55.

3. Seward memorandum, March 29, Scott memorandum, March 30, Scott to Lincoln, April 1, 1861, in the R. T. L. Collection; *Collected Works*, IV, 320; *Official Records*, ser. I, vol. I, pp. 363–65; *Official Records of the Union and Confederate Navies in the War of the Rebellion* (26 vols., 1894–1922), ser. I, vol. IV, p. 109; M. C. Meigs, "Diary, March 29–April 8, 1861," in the *American Historical Review*, XXVI (1920–21), 299–301; Bancroft, *Seward*, II, 129; D. D. Porter, *Incidents and Anecdotes of the Civil War* (1885), pp. 13–16; Nevins, *Improvised War*, pp. 58, 60–61.

4. Aspinwall to Lincoln, March 31, 1861, in the R. T. L. Collection; Fox, *Confidential Correspondence*, I, 12–18.

5. *Collected Works*, IV, 316–18; Bancroft, *Seward*, II, 116, 128–31; Nevins, *Improvised War*, pp. 62–63.

6. Letters to Lincoln from Neal Dow, March 13, O. Lovejoy, March 27, J. Blanchard, March 28, S. A. Allibone, March 29, O. B. Peirce, March 31, 1861, in the R. T. L. Collection; Nicolay and Hay, *Lincoln*, III, 423–28; A. B. Magruder, "A Piece of Secret History: President Lincoln and the Virginia Convention of 1861," in the *Atlantic Monthly*, XXXV (1875), 438–45; J. M. Botts, *The Great Rebellion* (1866), pp. 198–202; Shanks, *Secession Movement*, pp. 192–94; Bancroft, *Seward*, II, 120–21; W. L. Hall, "Lincoln's Interview with John B. Baldwin," in the *South Atlantic Quarterly*, XIII (1914), 268–69; Strong, *Diary*, I, 112; Randall, *Lincoln the President*, I, 326; B. P. Thomas, *Abraham Lincoln* (1952), p. 540. The testimony on the Lincoln-Baldwin interview is tangled and confusing. I have picked

my way through the evidence in the light of Fox's testimony in *Confidential Correspondence*, I, 38–41, which seems to give the best clue to what actually occurred.

7. *Official Records*, ser. I, vol. I, pp. 230–36; Fox, *Confidential Correspondence*, I, 12–14, 18–19, 38–41; Doubleday, *Reminiscences*, p. 135; Russell, *Diary* (Pratt ed.), pp. 35–37; Nicolay and Hay, *Lincoln*, IV, 28.

Chapter 4

1. Welles, *Diary*, I, 23–28; *Official Records*, ser. I, vol. I, pp. 240–41, 287, 368–70, 393–99; *Official Records, Navies*, ser. I, vol. IV, pp. 111–12; Meigs, "Diary," in *American Historical Review*, XXVI (1920–21), 301–2; Porter, *Incidents*, pp. 16–22; Russell, *Diary* (Pratt ed.), p. 115; Bancroft, *Seward*, II, 144–46.

2. Cameron to Anderson (in Lincoln's hand), April 4, 1861, in the R. T. L. Collection; *Collected Works*, IV, 323–24; Welles, *Diary*, I, 29–30; *Official Records*, ser. I, vol. I, pp. 236–37, 242–43, 245, 462–63; *Official Records, Navies*, ser. I, vol. IV, pp. 109–11, 125.

3. Botts, *Great Rebellion*, pp. 195–97, 257, 262, 270, 275–77.

4. Scott to Lincoln, April 5, 8, 9, C. P. Stone to Seward, April 5, Fox to Blair, April 8, 1861, in the R. T. L. Collection; Fox, *Confidential Correspondence*, I, 26–27; *Official Records*, ser. I, vol. I, p. 241; Russell, *Diary* (Pratt ed.), pp. 40–45; Botts, *Great Rebellion*, pp. 114–15n.; Bancroft, *Seward*, II, 140–42; W. B. Hesseltine, *Lincoln and the War Governors* (1948), pp. 144–45; *Collected Works*, IV, 324.

Much has been made of a so-called "governors' conference" and its influence upon Lincoln's Sumter decision. During the first week in April, not only Governor Curtin of

Pennsylvania but also the governors of other Northern states called at the White House. On April 4 the Washington correspondent of the *New York Herald* wrote that Governors O. P. Morton of Indiana and Israel Washburne of Maine "had a long interview with the President today." These and other gubernatorial visits occasioned "much wild talk and guessing." (*Herald,* April 5, 8, 1861.) Undoubtedly the governors urged Lincoln to hold the Southern forts. Still, it appears that he was less interested in their views on Sumter and Pickens than in their readiness to provide state troops, which he thought were needed primarily for the defense of the national capital.

5. Letters to Lincoln from I. Underhill, April 2, W. H. West, April 3, "A Republican," April 3, J. H. Jordan, April 4, C. Schurz, April 5, G. F. Lewis, April 5, J. B. Stockton, April 8, "A member of the 7th Reg't National Guard," New York, April 10, 1861, all in the R. T. L. Collection; Strong, *Diary,* I, 114, 115, 117; H. C. Perkins, ed., *Northern Editorials on Secession* (2 vols., 1942), II, 703–4; Jay to Chase, April 4, 1861, in the *Annual Report of the American Historical Association for 1902,* II, 493; Russell, *Diary* (Pratt ed.), pp. 20–21; Gobright, *Recollections,* pp. 312–14; Tomes, *War with the South,* p. 167; Nevins, *Improvised War,* pp. 65–66.

6. H. B. Small to Lincoln, April 2, Cameron to Anderson (with Lincoln's endorsement), April 4, Chew to Lincoln, April 8, Scott to Lincoln, April 10, 1861, in the R. T. L. Collection; *Collected Works,* IV, 324; *Official Records,* ser. I, vol. I, pp. 251–52; Bates, *Diary,* pp. 181–82; Russell, *Diary* (Pratt ed.), pp. 45–47.

Chapter 5

1. *Official Records*, ser. IV, vol. I, pp. 104–6; Russell, *Diary* (Pratt ed.), p. 93; De Leon, *Four Years*, pp. 23–29, 37, 39–40; Rhodes, *History*, III, 299–300; Davis, *Rise and Fall*, I, 230, 607–8; Stampp, *And the War Came*, p. 82.

2. Hurlbut to Lincoln, March 27, 1861, in the R. T. L. Collection; J. L. Pugh to W. P. Miles, January 24, 1861, in the Miles MSS., Southern Historical Collection, University of North Carolina; John McRae to J. and J. D. Kirkpatrick, December 29, 1860, in the McRae MSS., State Historical Society of Wisconsin; Perkins, *Northern Editorials*, I, 220; Dumond, *Southern Editorials*, pp. 313–14, 353–54, 418–19, 462–63; *Official Records*, ser. I, vol. I, p. 447; ser. IV, vol. I, pp. 122–23, 151; Edward McPherson, *The Political History of the United States of America during the Great Rebellion* (1865), p. 112; Greeley, *American Conflict*, I, 415n., 450–51; De Leon, *Four Years*, pp. 26–27; White, *Rhett*, pp. 192–93, 197, 200–203; Russell, *Diary* (Pratt ed.), pp. 37–40, 87; Nicolay, *Outbreak*, pp. 69–71; *Annual Report of the American Historical Association for 1911*, II, 543–44, 555; De Leon, *Four Years*, p. 35; Colton, *Western Territories*, pp. v–vi; Swanberg, *First Blood*, pp. 288–89; Hudson Strode, *Jefferson Davis* (2 vols., 1955–59), II, 39.

Much of this ground has been covered by R. N. Current, "The Confederates and the First Shot," in *Civil War History* (December, 1961), pp. 357–69.

3. *Official Records*, ser. I, vol. I, pp. 26, 82, 119, 258–60, 283, 447, 451, 454; ser. IV, vol. I, pp. 61–68, 87, 165; *Annual Report of the A. H. A. for 1911*, II, 558; Davis, *Rise and Fall*, I, 311; Bancroft, *Seward*, II, 118–19; Nicolay, *Outbreak*, pp. 43–44; Nicolay and Hay, *Lincoln*, III, 413; IV, 18–19; Rhodes, *History*, III, 328.

NOTES

4. *Official Records,* ser. I, vol. I, pp. 283–91, 456–57; Bancroft, *Seward,* II, 141; Nicolay, *Outbreak,* p. 79.

5. *Official Records,* ser. I, vol. I, pp. 13–14, 18, 29, 31, 54, 60, 290, 292–94, 297, 299, 300–2, 304, 459–61; Dumond, *Southern Editorials,* pp. 446, 482–83, 485–86; Perkins, *Northern Editorials,* II, 705–6; Greeley, *American Conflict,* I, 632; Doubleday, *Reminiscences,* pp. 140–41; Rhodes, *History,* III, 297–99, 348–50; Nevins, *Improvised War,* pp. 67–70, 73.

Chapter 6

1. *Collected Works,* IV, 329–31; Bates, *Diary,* pp. 182–84; Strong, *Diary,* I, 118; Nicolay, *Outbreak,* pp. 73, 83–84; Nicolay and Hay, *Lincoln,* IV, 72.

2. Strong, *Diary,* I, 118–22; De Leon, *Four Years,* p. 36; Botts, *Great Rebellion, pp.* 113, 201–2, 205–7; Greeley, *American Conflict,* I, 453n., 459n.; Tomes, *War with the South,* p. 159; Shanks, *Secession Movement,* pp. 202–4; White, *Rhett,* p. 205; Nicolay, *Outbreak,* pp. 76–77.

3. Schurz, *Reminiscences,* II, 227–30; Nicolay, *Outbreak,* pp. 78, 84, 87, 91–92, 98–99, 103; Nicolay and Hay, *Lincoln,* IV, 159; Botts, *Great Rebellion,* pp. 113–14n.; Lutz, in *Annual Report of the A. H. A. for 1915,* pp. 211–13.

4. *Official Records,* ser. I, vol. I, pp. 11, 16–25, 374–76, 406–7; *Official Records, Navies,* ser. I, vol. IV, p. 132; Fox, *Confidential Correspondence,* I, 31–38, 42–44; Nicolay and Hay, *Lincoln,* IV, 56.

5. *Collected Works,* IV, 423–27, 441; *The Diary of Orville Hickman Browning,* ed. by T. C. Pease and J. G. Randall (2 vols., 1925–33), I, 476; *Messages and Papers of the Confederacy,* ed. by J. D. Richardson (2 vols., 1905), I, 63–75; Davis, *Rise and Fall,* I, 263–81; Perkins, *Northern Edi-*

torials, I, 381; Russell, *Diary* (Pratt ed.), p. 191; Nicolay, *Outbreak,* pp. 79–80, 105–6; Nicolay and Hay, *Lincoln,* III, 411; IV, 36, 254–55; Bancroft, *Seward,* II, 146–48.

Chapter 7

1. Randall, *Lincoln the President,* I, 343; *Mississippi Valley Historical Review,* XXVIII (1941), 72–73; T. J. Pressly, *Americans Interpret Their Civil War* (1954), p. 65; Stephens, *Constitutional View,* II, 34–36, 349; Davis, *Rise and Fall,* I, 292, 294, 297.

2. T. M. Anderson, *The Political Conspiracies Preceding the Rebellion, or the True Stories of Sumter and Pickens* (1882), pp. 57–58; Nicolay and Hay, *Lincoln,* IV, 33, 44–45, 62–63; Ramsdell, "Lincoln and Fort Sumter," in the *Journal of Southern History,* III (1937), 259–88; Tilley, *Lincoln Takes Command* (1941), pp. 139–48, 262, *passim.*

3. Randall, "Lincoln's Sumter Dilemma," in the *Abraham Lincoln Quarterly,* I (1940), 3–42, reproduced in Randall, *Lincoln the Liberal Statesman* (1947), pp. 88–117; Randall, *Lincoln the President,* I, 311–50; Potter, *Lincoln and His Party,* pp. 315, 320, 326, 358–59, 363–67, 374–75; K. M. Stampp, "Lincoln and the Strategy of Defense in the Crisis of 1861," in the *Journal of Southern History,* XI (1945), 297–323; Stampp, *And the War Came: The North and the Secession Crisis* (1950), pp. 263–86.

4. Potter pointed out Tilley's error before 1947; see *Lincoln and His Party,* pp. 333–35. See also Stampp, *And the War Came,* p. 264n.

5. Randall, *Liberal Statesman,* p. 109.

6. Randall, *Lincoln the President,* I, 350.

7. Potter, *Lincoln and His Party,* pp. 315, 363–67; Randall, *Liberal Statesman,* pp. 98–101. Randall says in *Lincoln the*

President, I, 316: "Pickens was susceptible of adjustment. Sumter, on the other hand, was packed with psychological dynamite." The evidence certainly does not bear out this view. Though Sumter received the greatest immediate attention both North and South, Pickens was also packed with psychological dynamite, and the situation there, already explosive enough, would have remained explosive even if, somehow, the Sumter issue had been disposed of. Curiously, Nicolay and Hay, *Lincoln,* III, 427, accept the idea of the Sumter-for-Pickens alternative as Lincoln's, even though this is inconsistent with other evidence they present, if not indeed inconsistent with their overall treatment of the Sumter question.

8. Compare Ramsdell, *Journal of Southern History,* III, 278, and Stampp, *And the War Came,* p. 178, both of whom stress April 4 rather than April 6 as the crucial date.

9. *Lincoln and His Party,* pp. 374–75. Both Potter and Randall read their own conclusions into Lincoln's inaugural. They give the impression that Lincoln promised to refrain from using force. Randall goes so far as to omit the qualifying phrase, "beyond what may be necessary for these objects," in quoting Lincoln's statement that he intended "no invasion, no using of force." *Liberal Statesman,* p. 115. See Stampp, *And the War Came,* p. 200.

10. W. E. Dodd, *Statesmen of the Old South* (1911), pp. 220–21.

11. See also Current, in *Civil War History* (December, 1961), pp. 368–69. Nevins, *Improvised War,* 67–74, redresses the balance. Nevins remarks, p. 74n., that the efforts of the Ramsdell school may well be left "to fulfill their presumed purpose of comforting sensitive Southerners." Apparently the Ramsdell thesis meets an emotional need.

12. *Collected Works,* VIII, 332.

INDEX

Index

INDEX

Index

INDEX

Index